ARCHITECTURAL PLANTS & PLANTING

ARCHITECTURAL PLANTS & PLANTING

SUNNIVA HARTE

NEW HOLLAND

This paperback edition published in 2003.

First published in 2001 by
New Holland Publishers (UK) Ltd
London • Cape Town • Sydney • Auckland

Garfield House, 86 Edgware Road
London W2 2EA
United Kingdom

80 McKenzie Street
Cape Town 8001
South Africa

Level 1, Unit 4
14 Aquatic Drive
Frenchs Forest, NSW 2086
Australia

218 Lake Road
Northcote
Auckland
New Zealand

10 9 8 7 6 5 4 3 2 1

ISBN 1 84330 466 X

Editor: Christine Rista
Design: Roger Hammond
Production: Caroline Hansell
Editorial Direction: Rosemary Wilkinson

Reproduction by PICA Colour Separation, Singapore
Printed and bound in Singapore by Tien Wah Press
(Pte) Ltd

With thanks to my daughter,
Rebecca Masterton,
for her unfailing love and
support.

CONTENTS

INTRODUCTION

ALL GARDENS, no matter what their size or location, have the power to arouse the emotions: excitement, pleasure, contentment and happiness. Architectural plants are among the gardener's most powerful tools in creating a magical space that is simultaneously physically relaxing and mentally invigorating, vitally important attributes to anyone living a highly pressured modern life. With the intelligent use of appropriate plants, a garden can be made into an enchanted space that has a powerful 'energy', rejuvenating anyone who lingers within its boundaries.

Architectural plants are also designer plants, with a definite shape and a strong form; they make up the skeleton of the garden, its structure. They usually have well-defined foliage and their inherent outline helps to strengthen and balance the overall design of the largest or smallest of plots, bringing out the best in nearby plants. Used with care, designer plants help to define the framework of a garden: without them the whole could easily become a blurred, soft-focus expanse.

Opposite: The strongly sculptural leaves of an agave provide a visual focus while accentuating the gentle textural character of the long-stemmed lavender nearby. A small clay pot containing sempervivum holds the eye and balances the planting. The blues, mauves and greys of the planting create a feeling of coolness and harmony that is welcoming and restful in the heat of a hot Mediterranean garden.

Above: The bold, simple, striped leaves of canna lilies counterbalance the relaxed nature of the scarlet dahlias. The yellow and green leaves bring the scarlet flowers fully alive and at the same time emphasize the plummy blackness of the dahlia's leaves, so that together the two plants bring a dynamic vibrancy to their surroundings.

Architectural plants act much as punctuation marks do in a piece of prose. Without commas, full stops, semi-colons, exclamation marks and paragraphs as a guide, the reader would not know where to pause. Punctuation also indicates a change of subject or emphasis, and gives rhythm and energy to a piece of writing. Architectural plants perform more or less the same task in the garden. Placed in an intelligent way, they make it possible to 'read' the design. If a plot were filled only with plants of similar shape and size, there would be no visual signals to direct the gaze to places at which to pause. By using key plants at strategic points, the gardener can devise the 'picture' he or she wishes to convey, and guide the eye from one area to another, an essential tool in garden design.

Right: Key visual points have been placed at intervals throughout this terraced garden so that the eye is led from one area up and onto another. Box balls and terracotta urns hold the garden together, giving it a cohesive feeling. Ivy-covered walls add a sense of stability and solidity as does the columnar-shaped group of trees, which also adds important vertical interest to this sunny, warm garden.

An architectural plant has a clear shape. Be it a tree, shrub, climber, perennial or annual, it must have a strong, simple outline to counterbalance other plants with a more haphazard style of growth. A roadside signpost has to be simple and has to be placed in the right position to perform its task; the same can be said of designer plants. For this reason they tend to be larger than any other plants surrounding them, which also helps to create a sense of scale, giving the plot height and breadth.

In order for the garden and its planting to have cohesiveness, this sense of scale or proportion is required throughout the plot. Different heights and widths of plants are also necessary to create variety. Height carries the eye upwards and gives the illusion of greater space. This attribute is especially important in small or enclosed spaces, where it may be needed to counterbalance a tall blank wall that could be over-dominant. However, if the same wall is clothed in leaves it recedes somewhat, and any variations in leaf colour add a positive note. A wild meadow, made up mainly of horizontals, can be made more three-dimensional by planting one or more well-shaped trees. Without the

trees, the eye would glide quickly over the flower-studded grass, and the individual beauty of the flowers would be dissipated. But the vertical of the tree will balance the horizontal expanse of grass, and each will draw out the best characteristics of the other.

Playing with space and scale can add greatly to the visual harmony of a garden. Scale is more easily understood if the eye has

a focal point, while space can be controlled with defined areas of planting. Shaped and trimmed hedges or broad swathes of one type of plant will help to 'compartmentalize' a garden. Position low contoured hedges and espalier fruit trees to draw the eye along a path or define the area of a vegetable garden. A broad conical tree, planted a third of the way across a narrow garden will give the illusion of greater width, while blue-grey lavender, grown in neat close rows on a hillside, emphasizes the contours of the land.

Tall architectural plants are invaluable for providing a link between the garden and its buildings as well as with the surrounding landscape. They can also be used to link one area of a garden to another. A country garden is often composed of different areas.

Right: Bold spiky leaves of agave add drama and style to this French garden, which is composed almost entirely of shrubs and trees. The interest and excitement is provided by mixing together well-shaped shrubs of various green tones. The dense dark-green fir trees act as a wonderful foil to the airiness of the yuccas, palms and agaves.

Above: Espalier apple trees make a wonderful living wall between one area of the garden and another. Behind them a brick wall is partially disguised with beautifully trained fruit trees which reinforce the height of the wall while visually breaking the monotony of it.

Right: The strength and classical beauty of this French villa is balanced with the judicious use of architectural plants. Generous box balls hold the eye before leading the gaze horizontally around the garden, while broadly columnar trees placed close to the house act as a link between it and the garden. The trees also partially screen the buildings, to create a feeling of secrecy and tranquillity.

If the same plant is grown in each section, the garden becomes tied together and united, rather as a thread joins different beads together to form a necklace. Weaving the same plant in and out of different areas gives the whole area a feeling of stability.

Plants with a strong character are invaluable for counterbalancing and emphasizing the architecture of nearby buildings. An imposing Italian villa, for example, would look incongruous surrounded by a cottage garden. The strong lines of the building would dominate and overpower the delicate shapes of soft, pretty flowers like geranium, larkspur and Oriental poppies, and their beauty would be dissipated. Dominant buildings require plants that can match their strength and form: dark, sculptural yews (*Taxus baccata*) and tall columns of Italian cypresses with their distinctive, narrow shapes are not easily overwhelmed.

Small plants with distinctive, stylish, well-formed leaves and a well-defined outline can also be architectural. A really well-thought-out garden will have three-dimensional pockets of interest throughout, from eye-level to

ground-level. The attention given to small ground-level areas helps to build an overall picture that has depth of interest; the more interest a garden has the more enduring it becomes. For example, a hedge composed of a single shrub will be enhanced when small plants, such as *Arum italicum*, with well-shaped leaves, are planted at its base, thereby providing a foreground which balances the uniformity of the hedge behind. All gardens become more dynamic when key plants are used to signal the background, middle and foreground.

Architectural plants can be used to complement plants with softer shapes, each drawing out the best qualities of the other. The charms of a herbaceous border planted up with perennials and annuals is transient, as most of them have died down in winter.

Architectural plants, such as Cardoon (*Cynara cardunculus*) or clipped box (*Buxus sempervirens*), are vital for keeping a sense of life and energy throughout the dull winter months. Their role is not confined to the winter, however; in summer, when the flowering plants mingle together in billowing clouds, these stalwarts tie the planting together, giving it unity and strength. Those much-needed attributes are vital to a garden, bringing a sense of tranquillity and calm that is all too rare in the busy world we live in.

It is possible to capitalize on accepted associations between plant and place to create a sense of drama and excitement. Large paddle-leaved Japanese banana plants (*Musa basjoo*) are synonymous with humid, sunny tropical countries where deep jungles clothe the mountainsides - translated into a

Right: This small area overflows with different textural elements. The dominant forked tree trunk is balanced by the diagonally placed flagstones and the strong and distinctive leaf shapes of clivia, with its smooth strap-shaped leaves, *Ligularia stenocephala*, with its serrated leaves, and the smooth-edged leafed *Ligularia* 'Gregynog Gold'.

Above: Neat rosettes of succulents blend with the pebbles and rocks in this dry garden, their shapes changing little throughout the seasons. As a consequence, you can create semi-permanent patterns with them, carpeting the ground in a decorative manner.

town garden, they instantly give the allure of a tropical oasis. In cool climates the town gardener has greater scope for experimentation, as towns are generally two or three degrees warmer than country gardens. You can opt for a Mediterranean style, where plants are tough enough to survive long dry summers and cool winters. Many grey-leafed plants, such as sage, lavender and santolina, which originated in

Above: The distinctive yellow and green striped leaves of *Canna* 'Striata' make an effective series of verticals amongst the decorative blue-grey leaves of *Melianthus major*. The hot-orange canna flowers contrast with the sugar-pink flowerheads of cleome, thereby creating a tropical atmosphere in this sheltered, cool-climate lush garden.

Mediterranean countries, retain their leaves throughout the winter and can withstand a certain amount of neglect. They are ideal for gently snipping into shapes to provide focal points amongst summer bedding plants and are also suitable for edging paving to introduce a light formality to a simple design.

Alternatively why not create a miniature 'Italian-style' haven in which low box hedges enclose mixed flowering plants; as a counterpoint, position handsome standard bay trees in large terracotta pots symmetrically alongside a path or beside a seating area. Equally, a seaside-style garden could be recreated by planting simple low-growing coastal plants such as *Crambe maritima* and various sedums in an expanse of shingle. Strategically positioned pieces of driftwood and large pebbles would complete the picture. This kind of garden looks best against a wide expanse of sky.

Gardens should provide a positive emotional experience, and the planting itself can contribute to its character. Structural shrubs and herbaceous plants with a rounded shape are soothing and infuse a garden with gentleness. Angular, spiky or pointed plants are more dynamic and energetic. They are useful for adding balance to a garden, especially when it is full of billowing rounded shapes and perhaps surrounded by undulating hills. Climbers trained up and around an obelisk act as exclamation marks or vertical points.

A sense of mystery can be added by obscuring the garden perimeter and the area beyond with thick planting. Use tall thickets of different bamboos that swish and rustle in the breeze on either side of a meandering path to prevent the full expanse of the garden from being seen at a single glance. In a confined space, the bamboos would appear taller than they actually are, giving the impression of a mysterious but managed jungle.

Humour can be introduced in a garden with the use of architectural and sculptural objects as well as with topiary birds and animals. Even everyday objects become

Above: Humour lightens the mood of a garden. The owner of this hedge has made it more interesting and less sedate by clipping it into the shape of a giant half-hidden cat. Topiary gives you, the gardener, ample opportunity to follow your imagination and so make your garden unique and memorable.

humorous when used in an unexpected way; a large yew topiary animal set amongst conservative plantings of perennials and shrubs, or a metal dog peeking out from beneath a cascade of clematis, for example. A willow figure seated beside a pond or garden building humanizes the area while introducing a sense of scale and interest. The size of the figure provides a means of measuring its surroundings and its gaze directs the visitor to look in the same direction and thereby notice a fine view or noteworthy planting that might otherwise have been missed.

When architectural plants and objects are chosen and positioned with care and consideration they enliven and personalize a garden. With greater emphasis on balanced horizontals and verticals, and a greater depth of field, the garden makes a positive statement without losing harmony, giving all who visit it an infinitely greater sense of contentment and pleasure.

Every garden is a unique experience, but the strength, impact and pleasure of the experience it offers depends on its style, in which the judicious placing of designer plants and sculptural elements plays a major part. Gardens with a coherent, tangible style are more memorable, enticing the visitor to return time and time again.

Big, bold, striking plants or plant groups are key elements in creating a distinctive style. Large, lush plants massed together in a confined city space will surprise, excite and delight. Neatly clipped yew and box hedges in ordered shapes create a still, tranquil mood that encourages the imagination and jogs the memory of peaceful times when days stretched lazily ahead.

Use such architectural, designer plants in various ways to create different moods and settings. They should never overpower or dominate their surroundings but should bind elements of the garden together to create a wonderful uplifting space.

1
Putting style into the garden

Left: This damp and shady area is lightened by a large clump of low-growing symphytum; its lemon-edged leaves contrast sharply with the large circular dark green leaves of ligularia behind them, and the stylish leaves of rodgersia across the path. Variegated hosta in the background provides additional pools of light.

CLASSICAL ITALIAN GARDENS

Bathed in intense light, classical Italian gardens appear positive yet composed. They rely on a few well-shaped evergreens, formal pools and wide gravel paths for structure and style, a concept that can easily be recreated in areas of the world with a broadly similar climate. The repetitive geometric use of evergreens creates harmony and offers interest throughout the year, providing a refined and elegant backdrop for classical architecture, while also encouraging a feeling of calm and timelessness. Renaissance thinkers believed that a garden of this sort provided the ideal environment for humanists to concentrate on philosophical, as opposed to physical, preoccupations.

Above: The positive and distinctive style of this Italian villa is complemented by the simple but strong design of the garden that surrounds it. Broad, low, clipped box hedges echo the architectural lines of the house. Larger clipped box shapes provide height and break up the line of vision, making the area feel larger than it actually is.

Simplicity is the keynote of these handsome gardens, and the Italians are masters at using it to create a powerful theatrical experience. Tall solid hedges, curved and shaped into elegant lines, offset to perfection a beautiful antique stone bench or an urn planted with a cascade of roses. These hedges contribute to a sense of romance; they can also be used to create small enclosures or 'cabinets', the ideal settings for secret trysts; they are ideally suited to large exposed sites, as their living green walls shelter both people and plants from biting winds, even on the coldest day.

The pencil-slim, tall, evergreen Italian cypress (*Cupressus sempervirens*) is strongly associated with the Italian rural landscape, so much so that its introduction into a garden at once brings a Mediterranean flavour to it.

Cypresses make valuable trees, as they provide strong, simple vertical lines; they are ideal positioned in a parterre close to a house, as their height links the nearby building with the garden. In a hillside location, a levelled *allée* of tall, dark, Italian cypresses leading to a view will create a theatrical atmosphere.

Many Italian gardens feature wide gravel paths that run between waist-high, neatly clipped hedges of box or yew. Spaces behind the hedges are sometimes planted with spherical or conical standards of citrus trees to act as focal points within the overall design. The heady scent of their spring blossom wafts through the walkways, delighting the senses of any visitor wandering along them. In colder climates you could achieve a similar design by substituting hardy evergreens for the orange or lemon trees, particularly slow-growing shrubs and trees with small leaves that are easy to shape. Holly (*Ilex*), *Viburnum tinus*, Portugal laurel *(Prunus lusitanica)* and box *(Buxus sempervirens)* are all suitable. They can be planted at intervals in the ground, or in pots, to emphasize the classical lines of the architecture.

Box and yew parterres can be reproduced with great success in even quite small gardens. They can be designed to fit any shape and bring a sense of purpose to a plot. The Italians love to fill their parterres with brilliantly coloured flowers, in strong contrast with the dark green of the shrubs. In windy sites the low hedges protect the flowers and keep them upright; furthermore, the exuberant growth of the infill flowers acts as a counterpoint to the formality of the parterre.

Left: A classical pillar placed at one side of this path adds a romantic touch to the garden and draws the eye before leading it onto the discreetly placed wooden bench placed in the cool shadows. Low box balls add a feeling of refinement to an otherwise casual planting of lavender and honeysuckle.

Above: A false perspective has been given to this small rectangular area by planting tall yews at the outer edge of the area and progressively smaller ones towards the wall. The gravel walk is narrower at the rear than it is at the front, reinforcing the illusion that the area is twice as long as it actually is.

COASTAL GARDENS

Coastal gardens exposed to salt-laden winds often have an informal style of planting that blends in well with the surrounding seascape. In such gardens it is important to introduce some designer, architectural plants into the overall scheme to give the whole an element of structure. This will help to anchor the garden to the surrounding landscape and provide a contrast to the wildness of the elements that buffet it.

Above: Tresco Abbey gardens on the Isles of Scilly are proof that salt-laden winds are no deterrent to creating a garden that is both dynamic and beautiful. Stone walls retain the sun's warmth, while making an ideal home for *Lampranthus haworthii*, which adds a vibrant splash of colour at the feet of a perfectly shaped *Dasylirion*.

Many coastal gardens are sited on the edge of cliffs and are steeply sloping. This makes maintenance a real problem, and it is all the more important that a planting scheme is devised that does not need constant titillating. Mound-forming alpine plants do well in these circumstances. Sea thrift (*Armeria maritima*), with its dense green mounds of short grass-like leaves and pink globular flowers, enjoys the hard living to be had in rocky seaside gardens. Where the winters are not too severe agaves and sempervivums will grow happily amongst rocky outcrops, as their tough leaves are slower to lose moisture than those of more thin-skinned specimens.

Many native seaside plants have long taproots which delve deep among the pebbles. Such plants are designed to require little soil but others, such as roses, aquilegia and *Knautia macedonica*, need the help of fibrous compost. Many plants will adapt themselves to the strong winds by hugging the shingle and producing shorter flower stems.

It pays to remember that a shingle garden offers similar growing conditions to mountain regions: open and free-draining. Knowing the origins of a plant can help the gardener in his choice of plants. Small tulips, such as *Tulipa violacea* and *T. tarda*, that originate from Asia and the Turkish mountains, do well in shingle as they appreciate warmth in summer and the free-draining nature of their adopted environment.

Even in cool climates, a seaside garden can play host to a surprisingly wide variety of

Opposite: Yellow-flowered sea poppies, low mounds of erigeron, crinkled leaves of *Crambe maritama* and tall clumps of *Centranthus rubra* flower profusely on this shingle garden. Various interestingly shaped pieces of driftwood have been placed upright to add height and substance to the casual planting that is entirely in keeping with the seascape beyond.

plants. Roses, poppies, aquilegia, anthemis, bearded iris and osteospermum, all thrive near the sea, but their silhouettes tend to be soft and amorphous. Architectural plants with large distinctive leaves will help to pull the more informal plants together. *Helleborus argutifolius*, with its beautiful, thick, well-defined leaves, looks its best among marjoram (*Origanum*) or sage (*Salvia*

officinalis), for example. On a pebble beach garden, *Crambe maritima* comes into its own among poppies and ground-hugging saxifrages. Its wonderful silver-blue crinkled leaves hug the ground, making large, billowing mounds that increase in size as the years blow by. Their shape and colour seem ideally suited to growing under coastal wide open skies.

COTTAGE GARDENS

The cottage garden, much loved the world over, is renowned for its distinctive and dense planting of herbaceous perennials and annuals. Mixed massed plantings of geranium, iris, anthemis, sage and poppies are very vivid, but they can also easily become an indistinguishable haze of colours. More strongly defined elements help to inject some structure into the whole scheme, and provide strong vertical and horizontal features that remain constant throughout the changing seasons.

Right: The gardens at Great Dixter, in Sussex, England, are renowned for their bold and imaginative plant combinations. Here, *Kniphofia uvaria* 'Nobilis' stands majestically behind scarlet-flowered *Crocosmia* 'Lucifer'. Tall dark maroon seedheads of *Atriplex hortensis* var. *rubra* emphasize the vertically growing flowerheads of the kniphofia.

The smaller the cottage garden, the more important it is to plant it up in a series of layers. This has the effect of slowing the eye down as it travels from the plants nearest to you, to those in the middle distance and beyond. Each area can be differentiated by planting a tree, shrub or perennial with a distinctive and noticeable shape. To infuse the garden with a feeling of continuity, use the same distinctive plant in each section and separate them from each other with a range of typical cottage garden plants. In the foreground, low-growing viola and ajuga could be punctuated with tall white foxgloves, in the centre area plant aquilegias with pink and white foxgloves, while in the background opt for a mixture of old-fashioned roses and low-growing shrubs again with foxgloves, this time in deep pink.

It is important to have at least three distinctive shrubs or trees in a cottage garden to provide valuable winter interest, as many perennials die down in the cold months. A garden always looks more relaxed when an odd number of key plants are used; symmetrical planting on the other hand lends formality to a plot. Holly (*Ilex*) is a traditional cottage-garden plant and comes in many different forms. Some have leaves that are almost black; others are splashed or margined with yellow or cream. Holly grows happily in almost any situation and can either be left unpruned to grow into a shrub or small tree with a bare trunk, or it can be cut into a pleasing shape. Just three different varieties, planted at intervals (maybe placed on the tips of an imaginary triangle) will hold the plot of a small cottage garden together, giving it a feeling of substance.

In gardens protected from high winds, you can choose from a wide range of structural plants to provide these punctuation marks. Bear's breeches (*Acanthus mollis*), with its dark, glossy, cut-edged leaves and stiff, white and plum-coloured flower spikes, is ideal. Its clump of large leaves will help to anchor a constantly changing mass of

flowers. Great mullein (*Verbascum thapsus*) or *V. bombyciferum*, with large rosettes of ground-hugging woolly silvery leaves and tall spires of small yellow flowers, are ideal for creating vertical accents among a pavement planting, or in a bed of ground cover plants such as dianthus; their downy leaves are wonderful in the early morning when covered with thousands of dew droplets.

In small cottage gardens, transient sculptural plants can be used to alter the balance and feel of the plot from one year to the next, so that it never becomes dull. Mountain spinach (*Atriplex hortenseis* var. *purpurea*) is an excellent example. This fast-growing annual can easily be grown from seed, and its deep maroon leaves are well shaped and cover the tall stems, adding dramatic highlights in a mixed planting of perennials and annuals. It could also be grown to make a powerful colour statement among large clumps of scarlet-flowered red-hot pokers (*Kniphofia*).

Above: Neatly clipped low hedges of box counterbalance the relaxed nature of the herbs growing in this enclosed cottage garden. Their uniformity adds an air of permanence as well as a feeling of tranquillity and harmony to the area, all hallmarks of an English cottage garden.

WILD GARDENS

A wild garden is primarily one of indigenous plants; if these are not interspersed with strong architectural plants, the resulting planting lacks impact and definition. Strategically placed structural shrubs and perennials will help give it strength of character and a more positive feel.

Opposite: The wonderfully contorted trunk of this ancient *Malus floribunda* acts as a beautiful focal point amongst a sea of *Epimedium pinnatum colchicum*. A clump of vibrantly green *Euphorbia palustris* reinforces the casual nature of the planting in this area.

Wild gardens, whose hallmark is simplicity, are becoming increasingly popular with environmentally-minded gardeners. Many butterflies can survive only if they are able to lay their eggs and feed on certain wild plants. Some of these wild plants might be quite insignificant-looking when grown singly but if allowed to grow in large drifts they have a more sculptural appearance. For instance, in Britain and Europe the Orange tip (*Anthocharis cardaamines*) feeds on the decorative white flowers of Garlic mustard (*Alliaria petiolata*), Lady's smock (*Cardamine pratensis*), and related plants such as Sweet rocket (*Hesperis matronalis*). When any of these plants are massed together, they enhance their surroundings.

Without careful thought and a sensitive approach, a wild garden can have an unappealing, ill-defined appearance. Strategically placed designer shrubs and perennials will give it strength of character and a positive feel. The simplicity is achieved by planting relatively few different plants.

Most wild life, whether birds or butterflies, requires nectar or seed-bearing plants, and the owner of the wild garden can easily provide appropriate trees, shrubs and plants that have something to offer. An old orchard, containing ancient apple, pear and plum trees pruned into pleasingly rounded shapes can be given a more natural wild appearance by allowing the grass to grow long, which seed-eating birds will appreciate. Long grass can be made more striking by planting single dark blue bulbous iris, such as *Iris xiphium*, randomly.

Distinctive designer plants should be used with subtlety in the wild garden. They should reinforce the tranquillity of the space without standing out from it. For this reason, it is best not to use a single specimen plant that is vastly different from other plants close by. If they are the right variety, roses look magical planted amongst grass studded with ox-eye daisies and other wild flowers. A hybrid tea, however, which has stiff stems and often perfectly shaped buds and flowers, would look out of place, whereas a rose with a lax, rounded form of growth, as have many of the old-fashioned centifolias, Gallica hybrids, damask mosses, Burnet hybrids and sweetbriars, would look enchanting. They would look entirely at home in a cool-climate wild garden in a way that a stiffly formal phormium or agave would not.

A meadow, however small, covered in native wild flowers, becomes even more alluringly romantic when the horizontal plane is broken by the vertical of a well-shaped small tree such as the Wedding cake tree (*Cornus controversa*), so-called because its layered branches, covered in creamy white and green leaves, create a tier-like effect. In a larger garden, *Sorbus aria* 'Lutescens', whose new leaves shimmer silver in spring, harmonizes well when grass-spangled with ox-eye daisies or golden buttercups. A tree or two brings a sense of balance by first drawing the eye to themselves and thereafter to the area surrounding them. Without them, your eye would tend to glide quickly over the area, and the smaller, ground-hugging plants would be missed or passed over.

MEDITERRANEAN GARDENS

A traditional Mediterranean garden, dry and hot, relies mainly on drought-tolerant grey-leaved plants. Many of the culinary herbs, such as sage (*Salvia*) for example, happily ride out both intense summer heat and cold winter nights.

Right: This beautifully designed garden is both sophisticated and tranquil thanks to the predominantly cool green, white and mauve colour scheme. The simple square beds containing loosely pruned citrus trees and the terracotta pots of blue-flowered agapanthus add a symmetry that is classical and harmonious. A long, low, clipped hedge of santolina complements the long-flowering 'Iceberg' rose.

Grey is a soothing colour, but unbroken swathes of it can look a bit dull, and a few contrasting sculptural plants will enliven the whole scheme. *Yucca gloriosa* is a good choice; its overall shape is circular, with dynamic, dark green, sword-shaped leaves, and tall flower spikes rising above in a mass of bell-shaped white flowers; it makes a stunning feature against the skyline or beside a colour-washed wall. The Honey flower (*Melianthus major*), which comes from South Africa, is another wonderful designer plant. It has magnificent leaves divided into sharply serrated or scalloped fingers, beautifully defined after rain, when the tiny water droplets cling to every point along the leaf's edge. Melianthus looks particularly good growing behind a clipped lavender (*Lavandula*) or beside a small-leafed evergreen shrub such as Sea buckthorn (*Hippophae rhamnoides*) or the variegated *Rhamnus alaternus* 'Argenteo Variegata' which set off the strong shape of its leaves.

Some architectural plants refuse to be ignored. Big thistles like *Echium simplex, E. candicans* and *E. wildpretii*, for example, have attractive grey leaves that are lance- or strap-shaped, but it is their enormous flower spikes, standing proudly to attention, that draw the eye. In groups, they add a real 'wow' factor to the planting; introduced singly, they can also provide an important focal vertical point.

As Mediterranean gardens are usually hot in summer, it is important to provide some welcome shade. A small grove of citrus trees, neatly pruned, can create a shaded seating area and the sweetly scented blossom certainly enhances the pleasure of sitting there. The illusion of coolness and restfulness can also be conjured up by growing plants that are predominantly blue, white and mauve, together with soft grey foliage. If plants are grown in rows, or blocks of colour,

they will strengthen this illusion.

In those areas of deeper shade, the large Cuckoo-pint (*Arum italicum*) adds a magical touch in autumn, with its well-defined tear-shaped creamy flower encased in a glossy spear-shaped leaf. In a loose planting of *Gladiolus illyricus* or Californian poppies (*Eschscholzia californica*), the tall, clump-forming *Euphorbia characias*, with its whorls of lime-green flowers, can be used to provide a strong solid shape.

Top: The haphazard scheme both in and surrounding this sunken garden has been given meaning and style by adding some well-shaped plants. Urns containing handsomely pruned evergreens draw the eye to the flight of stone steps, while additional specimen plants in containers, placed at intervals throughout the area, bring a feeling of balance to the garden.

Above: In the heat and dryness of this Mediterranean garden, low, clipped silver-grey hedges of santolina introduce a feeling of coolness in this enclosed space. Conical shaped bay trees and neatly trimmed yew provide strong vertical shapes amongst the numerous shrubs that add permanent interest to the area.

DRY GARDENS

As weather patterns change and climates become warmer, many plants native to Central America can be introduced to create desert-style gardens. These big succulents can be exciting as well as complementary to modern architecture, which is often composed of powerful horizontal and vertical lines.

Above: Powerful mountains provide a strong background to this desert garden, where the planting is dynamic in its simplicity. The clean architectural lines of the house are matched and complemented by tall palms and a wide variety of cacti and succulents that are entirely at home in this inhospitable landscape. The plants act as the perfect link between the untamed mountains and the sophistication of the building.

Desert plants tend to have strong, structural shapes. Agaves, with their rosettes of thick, fleshy, pointed leaves, look impressive and make a positive statement planted amongst low-growing succulents. They can also be used to act as an 'accent' plant when positioned beside a gateway or pathway (although you should bear in mind that they are quite spiky, and therefore place them accordingly). *Dasylirion*, a Mexican plant that is very similar to the yucca, has fine sword-like leaves and flower shoots twice its height; it adds an elegant touch to sun-parched gardens. The barrel cactus (*Echinocactus grusonii*) provides a solid round shape, and can grow up to 4m (13ft). It looks striking in a contemporary setting, as

Left: Hot, dry gardens need not be devoid of style and excitement. Barrel cacti planted densely amongst tall trichocereus create a strong visual picture that is highly individual. The shape and texture of the cacti gives them an animal-like quality, generating a surprising and delightful atmosphere.

does the tall slim cactus (*Cephlocereus senilis*) that can reach a height of l5m (50ft) if kept in dry conditions.

The environmentalist who owns a dry garden will not wish to plant anything that requires watering, but will want to rely on plants that take care of themselves during long periods of drought, such as cacti and succulents. Most of these have a prehistoric-looking appearance that usually presents a design challenge to gardeners from cooler climates, as their form of growth is highly sculptural and definite. The best solution is to place only a few choice plants in a minimalist, abstract way. For this reason, cacti and succulents are ideal for planting close to dynamic modern architecture.

In hot courtyard gardens, pots of different types of echeverias can be massed together to create a graphic, sculptural feature. Close inspection will reveal interesting differences in leaf colour and form: *Echeveria lilacina*, for example, has silvery-grey leaves, while those of *Echeveria agavoides* are green with maroon tips. Steps to a front or back door can be made more attractive by placing a pot with the tall-growing succulent Mother-in-law's tongue (*Sansevieria trifasciata* 'Laurentii') on each step, or the highly decorative, rich plum-coloured *Aeonium arboreum* 'Arnold Schwarzkopf' in a repeating group. The strong static shapes of succulents and cacti can be lightened by mixing them with small palms with frond-shapes leaves.

Above: This desert garden feels powerful and dynamic. Surrounding low-growing succulents anchor the agave and the tall columns of *Cereus forbesii* to the sun-baked earth and add valuable additional colour to the area.

JUNGLE GARDENS

More and more of us now travel to exotic destinations for our holidays, and, on our return, we often want to replicate aspects of what we have seen in our own back gardens. The smallest of city plots gives the opportunity to devise a personal Eden that it is possible to enter simply by stepping out of the back door. Jungle-style planting is especially suited to town locations, where the subtropical or half-hardy plants gain the benefit of greater protection from winds and from severe frosts, temperatures in the city tending to be a few degrees warmer than in the open countryside.

Right: Lush green palm fronds and ferns create a rich jungle-like atmosphere in this garden. The different textures and shapes of the various plants give the area a lively feel. Placing an oriental lantern amongst the foliage suggests that this verdant corner lies in the heat and dampness of some Asian country.

Handsome, lush, large-leafed plants massed together have the added advantage of being able to hide perimeter walls, blocking out unattractive buildings and at the same time creating a feeling of secrecy. Small jungle gardens often look best with just a meandering path leading to a paved seating area, making the need for a lawn obsolete.

Jungle plants grow in soil that is built up by decaying leaf matter falling onto it, so that digging is not necessary. With moisture-laden air and circulating dampness at the plant's feet, the only garden tool needed is a pair of secateurs. The warmer the climate in which you garden, the greater the choice you have of these exotic plants.

In cooler climates, a tropical effect can be created using hardy palms and other frost-tolerant large-leaved plants. The Chusan palm (*Trachycarpus fortunei*) is one such plant, and so is its relative, the Windmill palm, (*Trachycarpus lalisectus*); both have large evergreen fan-shaped leaves. Placed next to the hardy, clump-forming bamboo *Phyllostachys nigra*, with its exciting dark olive green, almost black, clums, and frost-tender canna lilies, with striped leaves of maroons, or yellows and greens, it makes a striking combination. The New Zealand flax, (*Phormium tenax*), with its long, slim, sword-shaped leaves is another good choice for the cool-climate jungle garden.

Naturally, if you have the option to overwinter tender tropical plants in a glass house, the choice of what you can grow is far wider. Christopher Lloyd transformed his traditional rose garden at Great Dixter, in the south-east of England, into a vibrant jungle garden sizzling with colour. Mixing banana plants with brilliant dahlias, stripy-leafed

Above: The unmistakable huge leaves of the Japanese banana plant (*Musa basjoo*) and the deeply cut leaves of *Tetrapanax papyrifera* growing in the small courtyard garden at Great Dixter in Sussex, England, transport the visitor to a seemingly jungle-like paradise, where the air is humid and the sun shines daily. The illusion is reinforced by the use of hot-coloured flowers planted thickly amongst the large feature plants.

cannas with tall purple-flowered *Verbena bonariensis*, bouganvillea, grey-leafed eucalyptus and a large-leafed paulownia, he has created a surprisingly tropical paradise in the heart of England's herbaceous-border gardening counties.

In temperate climates a wide choice of plants can be used to create a luxuriant atmosphere. Paulownia, left to its natural state, grows into a tall tree, but can be given a more exotic shape by cutting its branches back to the main stem each year. This stimulates it to produce much larger leaves than it otherwise would, apple green and truly sculptural. Palms add to the tropical feel. Some palms are trunk-forming, such as the King palm (*Archontophoenix cunninghamiana*), others are clump-forming, such as the Lady palm (*Rhapis*) and the Bamboo palm (*Chamaedorea*). To grow well most tropical plants need a lot of light; overcast grey days do not encourage them to grow. Young tropical plants like to be in dappled shade; in the wild they are protected from light which is too intense by being beneath their taller parent. When planning your tropical garden it is important you mimic this. The Mexican Blue palm (*Brahea armata*) is a decorative plant with silver-blue, stiff, fan-shaped leaves that can be used to bring height and style to the simplest of plots, especially when under-planted with agaves, *Clivia miniata* or canna lilies. If you vary the height of the planting in this way, the overall effect of the whole will be more stimulating.

Where there are high humidity levels all year round, the gardener can really go to town. The large arrow-shaped leaves of *Xanthosoma sagittifolium* (sometimes spotted with white) immediately transform an area into a verdant paradise. This feeling is reinforced when they are planted amongst tall, sculptural banana plants, palms or *Strelitzia nicolai*, with its beautiful paddle-shaped leaves. Massed together, these stylish designer plants create an environment that is lush, luxuriant and private.

JAPANESE GARDENS

Highly controlled, so much so that it remains visually the same from one year to the next, a Japanese garden is the very opposite of the charming confusion of a jungle garden. The design of a Japanese garden is complete from its conception, the epitome of refinement. Each plant in it is carefully chosen for its form and shape, and for the effect that shape will have on that of the plants next to it. The space between plants is very important as well.

The seasons in a Japanese garden are all-important. In spring, the cherry tree is much in evidence; it is thought to have a brave and indomitable character, as its blossom appears when there is still a risk of snow and hard frosts. Cherry trees usually have a naturally pleasing growth habit, and can be used to add structure to a plot. *Prunus x yedoensis* 'Ivensii' is a small tree with a weeping habit; in early spring its branches are smothered with fragrant white blossom; planted beside a pond, it acts as a visual link between the still waters and the surrounding garden. Where a vertical focal point is needed the vase-shaped *Prunus* 'Spire', with its soft pink flowers and brilliant autumn foliage, is perfect. In a narrow garden a spreading tree can help to create a greater feeling of width; either *Prunus* 'Mount Fuji' or *P.* 'Shirotae', with their large snow-white blossoms along dark horizontal branches, would bring a feeling of spaciousness as well as wonder and delight to the garden on a dull spring day.

A designer perennial ideal for the Japanese garden is the hosta. Some hostas have small delicate leaves; others have large leaves and form huge, well-defined, clumps. All bring simplicity and style to any planting. In a minimalist gravel garden, a handsome pot containing a distinguished hosta, such as the greyish-blue *Hosta sieboldiana* 'Elegans', is all that is needed to complete the tranquil mood of the plot. In a typical Japanese garden, where many pines are grown, the broad, ribbed leaves of the hosta contrast admirably with the fine dark needles of the pine. A clump strategically placed next to the pine's trunk links the hard knobbly bark of the trees to the softness of the surrounding moss-covered earth.

The Japanese are fortunate in having many varieties of acer growing naturally in their islands, so that they have become a key plant in the overall design of most of their gardens. Acers can vary in size from low, rounded shrubs to large trees that have a pleasing silhouette. Their leaves turn wonderfully vibrant and exciting reds, maroons and oranges in autumn, which gives them the added attraction of symbolizing the approach of winter. When they are planted amongst dark-leafed pines, they have the effect of accentuating the overall height, width and texture of the pine. In autumn, for a few short weeks, they transform an otherwise predominately green space into one that is alive with colour.

The Japanese tend to focus on detail, such as the way rain or dew glistens on a leaf, and many of the larger-leafed hostas have a corrugated, veined surface that holds water droplets in a magical way. A glistening bead of light enhances and beautifies the leaf.

Rain drops also look striking on the evergreen *Ophiopogon*, whose tufts of thick grass-like leaves make it an ideal accent plant. Grown at the foot of a handsome large rock or of a stone water basin, it

Opposite: The plants beside this pathway have all the qualities so desirable in a Japanese garden. The shaped pine suggests respectful old age and immortality, while the carefully clipped rhododendron and the box give the area a discreetly subdued atmosphere. Tall conifers in the background shut out the busy world beyond this tranquil enclosed spot.

complements the texture of the stone and helps to anchor it visually to the soil.

As Japanese gardens are not designed to evolve over the years but are expected to be 'complete' at their conception, many of their shrubs and trees are trained into permanent shapes that are strong and positive by clipping and pruning. Evergreen pines and box in particular lend themselves to becoming stylized replicas of trees depicted in Chinese paintings. Their branches are set at an angle to the main trunk and the leaves are clipped into dense oval shapes.

In true Japanese gardens, shrubs are sometimes used to recreate the outline of Mount Fuji. Low-growing *Euonymus fortunei* is a favourite plant for achieving this. Available in different leaf colours, it enables the gardener to perfectly depict this most favourite of mountains by growing a dark-leafed variety with a lighter-leafed one, the dark colour representing the mountain side and the lighter one the snow-capped summit.

The effect of rigid shrubs, of which there are often many in a Japanese garden, is softened by the introduction of various other architectural plants. Heavenly bamboo (*Nandina domestica*) produces clump-forming, unbranched stems straight from the ground which are topped with delicate bi-pinnate leaves. Bamboos are also ideal for this, and almost every Japanese garden has either a bamboo structure or a bamboo plant in it. All cultivated bamboos are evergreen, and as many are also frost-hardy, they will provide shape and style throughout the depths of winter.

Bamboos grow from rhizomes, and each stem will grow to its full height in one season. They are either clump-forming or have a running habit, and most gardeners choose to grow the former, as they have a more architectural shape and are not invasive like the latter. The hardy and distinctive *Semiarundinaria fastuosa* is clump-forming in cool climates. It grows mid-green canes (or culms), which are striped purple-brown, particularly when young, up to 7.5m (24ft) tall, making it a favourite choice for screening an area. On the other hand, *Phyllostachys vivax* 'Aureocaulis', which is also clump-forming in cool climates, is one of the loveliest bamboos, with tall, thick and erect golden yellow culms which turn temporarily red in the sunlight.

Above: The shrubs in this tiny garden have been chosen for their different leaf texture and size, so that the area feels larger than it actually is. The acers have been thinned out so that their delicate shape is revealed, and the camellias have been planted to give solid blocks of colour throughout the depths of winter.

Opposite: This pine has been pruned to remain the same beautifully contorted shape despite the passing decades. Its wonderfully gnarled bark complements the fresh green and delicate leaves of the nearby acer, which links it to the still dark waters that lie beneath it.

WOODLAND GARDENS

The uninitiated often think that a woodland garden requires hardly any management at all, and can be left to grow pretty much as it likes. However, if left to themselves, plants such as brambles move in and take over, and saplings self-seed; unless they are removed, the woodland garden will soon become less of a romantic glade and more of an impenetrable thicket. Gentle sunlight filtering through tall trees casts an air of magic and mystery, and retaining this ethereal quality, whilst preventing nature from taking over, requires careful planning and maintenance.

Left: Well-spaced clumps of variegated hostas give a sense of solidity to the mass planting of the delicately flowering *Epimedium* 'Grand Yenomoto' and white violas. The hostas provide valuable focal points in what would otherwise be a sea of dancing flowerheads. The epimedium leaves harmonize well with those of the hosta.

Opposite: In the protection of tall woodland trees a marvellous variety of foliage plants creates an unceasingly interesting picture. Clumps of ferns grow happily among smooth-leafed bergenia and spotted pulmonaria leaves, while strappy leafed phormiums counterbalance large gunnera leaves and distinctive tree ferns.

In a cold climate, a small glade can be planted with handsome ferns, such as the Ostrich fern (*Matteuccia struthiopteris*). Its erect, vase-shaped fronds, when caught in the sun's rays, give it a structural quality that contrasts well with plants with a more lax habit. Another strongly sculpted plant for shade and damp is rodgersia. It has highly decorative leaves that vary in colour from burnt sienna to green, depending on the species and variety grown. Rodgersia look particularly fine in spring, when native flowers such as bluebells bloom happily under the freshly unfurling leaves of overhead trees.

One of the best, but also one of the most difficult, plants to grow for the cool woodland garden is *Trillium sessile*, with its maroon three-petalled Art Nouveau-style flowers, and

Trillium grandiflorum, with white flowers. Notoriously slow to establish and propagate, their very individual character makes them well worth the effort.

Good architectural plants that colonize easily in a woodland glade are foxgloves (*Digitalis*). Once established as a colony, they form an army of vertical spires that emphasize the height and majesty of the surrounding trees. They are a valuable design plant in the natural garden and can be used to link a wild area with a cultivated one, looking as impressive amongst ferns as amongst roses.

When a wood is planted with very tall trees such as larch, birch, beech, ash and oak, it is possible to plant large shrubs around and beneath them, so creating a middle level between the trees and the ground-cover plants. Ancient rhododendrons allowed to grow to their full height and width look spectacular flowering in the gentle light of the overhead emerging leaf canopy. A carpet of bluebells surrounding them will mirror the blue spring sky above and have the effect of making their rounded shapes and the erect tree trunks really stand out.

When a woodland garden has relatively low ground-cover, the shape of the tree trunks becomes more noticeable, and therefore more important. Thought should be given to choosing large shrubs or trees that not only are well shaped but which have a single trunk or one that is well forked. Often planting three of the same variety together can enhance a tree trunk's beauty. Good specimens for this are *Betula utilis jacquemontii* 'Grayshill ghost' or *Betula ermanii*. In autumn when russet leaves thickly cover the ground around them, they become magically beautiful, especially if the white autumn-flowering crocus (*Colchicum speciosum* 'Album') is planted thickly amongst the fallen leaves. Planting one or two Paperbark maples (*Acer griseum*) or Winter's barks (*Drimys winteri*) that have a distinctive and decorative bark, amongst native trees in a wooded glade will provide undemanding

but interesting focal points that will bring a feeling of definition and cohesiveness to it.

The line between the discreetly and the obviously cultivated is a narrow one. The former will have a lazy and gentle atmosphere in which no single plant leaps out from its neighbours, but where each seems perfectly at home with its companions. The latter will be

Above: Beneath the canopy of a massive beech tree, a drift of bluebells makes a welcome splash of colour amongst the well-shaped *Hosta* 'Elata' leaves. The filtering sunlight catches and emphasizes the upward-pointing fern fronds so that they become key plants in the scheme.

less relaxed, and a choice tree or plant will look slightly incongruous and out of place. In fact, the aim should be to create a space where all plants seem perfectly at home. In a coastal area *Arbutus menziesii*, with evergreen leaves and a powerful, rich, cinnamon-red trunk, brings a positive strength to a mixed woodland to match the wilderness of nature.

2
Enhancing Designs with Architectural Plants

W E LIVE IN A VISUAL AGE: colour is used to attract us. However, when it comes to creating a well-designed garden, it is sometimes necessary to resist the seductive charms of a well-known plant sporting a new colour, and instead find out what its overall shape is going to be once it is established. Will it form a thick, ground-hugging mound, or will it be low growing, with a haphazard way of spreading, so that once its flowers are over it has little to recommend it? If dealing with a tall perennial or a shrub, will it have a clearly defined shape or one that can be sculpted? These are very important considerations, and luckily most plants are now being sold with a brief description of their chief characteristics. The aim when putting plants together should be to bring out their best qualities and therefore to make them shine.

Left: A group of silver-leafed *Verbascum olympicum* growing in this dry gravel garden adds height, width and interest to the surrounding planting of euphorbia, eryngium and berberis. Their strong and simple shape gives the area an architectural quality that is refreshing, while their silver tones counterbalance the surrounding greens.

garden that relies mainly on flower colour for interest has an immediate visual impact, but it is one that quickly palls. When attention is paid to choosing and placing plants in it that are of varying heights, widths and forms, the impact is more permanent. However, it is not enough to grow a plant simply for its height or width. You need to also consider what companion plants should be grown close to it. In a small garden, where space is at a premium, this is vitally important. Choosing a small tree or shrub that has a trunk of maybe 1.8m (6ft) in height, such as Oriental thorn (*Crataegus laciniata* 'Ucria') or Fragrant snowbell (*Styrax obassia*), for example, allows the benefit of growing plants immediately beneath it.

Above: Without the use of verbascums and foxgloves this mixed border would appear simply as a haze of varying colours. The cream-coloured foxgloves add height and a sense of scale to the area, so that the wide range of flowering perennials is seen to better advantage.

Opposite: A typically English cottage planting of *Papaver orientale* and *Anthemis punctata* ssp. *cupaniana* is accentuated with a single plant of *Agave americana*. The variegated, strongly defined sword-like leaves of the agave create a visual shock which contrasts effectively with the informal and casual growth of its neighbours.

Opposite: Tall evergreen cypress trees placed at intervals throughout this garden bring a powerful feeling of height to this narrow space, thus making it feel larger. The additional planting of rounded ancient olive trees counterbalances their pencil-slim shapes. The strap-like leaves of the agapanthus disguise the base of the stone wall, providing much needed greenery at ground level.

Planting trees, shrubs and perennials that vary in their overall shape from one another gives a garden an energetic and vibrant feel. If the plants are all one shape, for example all spiky, such as foxgloves, delphiniums and erermurus, or all mound-forming, such as lavender, santolina, sedum and New Zealand hair sedge, the visual appeal will not be sustained.

Scale is also very important. A small space can be made to feel larger by planting key sculptural plants which are larger and better shaped than in the general planting, along an imaginary line through the garden. Sign post plants such as clipped bay and box, or nicely formed trees like standard apple and pear trees, take a visitor on a visual journey through the plot so that small

delectable plants close to them become all the more noticeable.

Informal gardens, such as cottage gardens, are characterized by the planting of a wide assortment of perennials that are often allowed to set seed where they will; many have soft-coloured flowers. The whole can appear a confusing jumble, unless it is anchored with a few choice sculptural points. Large-leafed grey and silver plants are highly decorative and ideal for this, in large and small gardens alike. The Scotch thistle (*Onopordum acanthium*), Globe artichoke (*Cynara scolymus*) or Cardoon (*Cynara cardunculus*), are all similar, and suit cool climate gardens where pale-pink Oriental poppies (*Papaver orientale*), ice-blue delphinium and white phlox grow. A sturdy clump of *Cynara cardunculus* in particular has the effect of heightening the delicate colours of flowers surrounding it, so that their shape is also better appreciated.

Mediterranean gardens can be vastly improved by including in the design plan some shrubs and trees that have a naturally distinctive shape. At the same time as providing good structural points, trees offer welcome shade from the unrelenting sunshine. Shrubs also give valuable shade and, together with trees, provide cooler growing spots for less sun-tolerant plants. Not all trees and shrubs naturally grow into a good shape and, even when they have the inclination, external factors might prevent their doing so. Strong winds howling over exposed sites bend, twist and contort. This can sometimes be beneficial; for example a tree that might otherwise have an untidy appearance can have its growth stunted so that it becomes more compact, even if somewhat asymmetrical.

Columnar-shaped evergreen trees, such as cypresses, are associated with dry Mediterranean gardens and, while they add important focal points, they do not provide shade. Eucalyptus are suited to dry

Above: A majestic thistle, *Onopordum acanthium*, rising above low-growing perennials, arrests the eye and in doing so draws attention to the plants at its feet. Its airy habit and distinguished height create a link between the flowering plants and the mature trees in the background.

conditions, but their extreme flammability makes them a hazard to be avoided in certain areas because of the danger of summer fires. The Edible olive (*Olea europaea* var. *europaea*) has a spreading, rounded crown of silver-grey evergreen leaves and a handsome trunk. Just one tree planted in an enclosed courtyard garden conveys a feeling of strength and stability, its gentle shape softening the hard angles of surrounding walls. Fully grown, it has a dignified character that becomes more pronounced if the paving beneath it is spangled with a self-willed annual such as the Californian poppy (*Eschscholzia californica*). Another tree for the warm, dry garden is the Santa Cruz ironwood (*Lyonothamnus floribunda* subsp. *aspleniifolius*) which originates from islands off California. It has a graceful shape with marvellous peeling chestnut-coloured bark and ferny evergreen leaves; since it grows to roughly 6m (20ft), it is ideally suited for a small plot where a vertical focal point is needed to counterbalance low-growing plants such as lavender and artemisia.

Right: The simple, uncluttered architecture of this Mediterranean villa is enhanced by the slender forms of perfectly grown Italian cypress trees. Their strong, dark personality acts as a counterpoint to the soft terracotta colour of the building. Profusely flowering angels' trumpets (*Brugmansia*), lighten the rigidity of the buildings and trees so that there is a feeling of grace and harmony throughout the area.

CREATING HORIZONTALS AND VERTICALS

The perspective of a garden can be manipulated by introducing various horizontal and vertical points within it, thus creating a feeling of scale; the scale of a plot in its turn can evoke different emotional responses. When planning where to put designer plants in a garden, the plot should first be treated as a whole, and then divided into three sections to give a foreground, middle distance and a horizon. If a garden lacks one of these it will feel unbalanced. Sculptural plants should be used to strengthen and emphasize each area, so that there is a feeling of cohesion to it. As they form the bones of the garden they should, where possible, be planted first, and perennials and annuals, which flower only briefly and do not have a distinctive silhouette, should be planted around them.

Opposite: This large clipped yew provides a solid vertical that will remain throughout the year and become increasingly important during the dormant winter months, when the nearby catalpa will have shed its leaves. The large golden catalpa leaves make a positive statement, their soft texture contrasting well with the spiky foliage of the yew.

A long, narrow garden predominantly featuring tall, vertically growing plants will feel confined and somewhat narrower than it actually is. A mass of verticals draws attention to the sky above. If a tree with horizontal growth is introduced, attention is drawn across as well as upward, thus helping to create the impression that the space is larger than it really is.

There are different ways to look at perspective and scale. The Japanese believe that you should design a garden to replicate nature, where anything viewed from a distance becomes smaller. In Japan a sense of distance is created by positioning the tallest plants nearest to the viewing point and the smaller ones at the back of a plot, whereas in the West large plants tend to be placed furthest away from the viewing point.

A minimalist city garden can be treated in the Japanese manner to create a sense of distance in a small enclosed space. The plot should be divided into three sections to give a foreground, middle ground and a distant point. If the entire area is paved or gravelled, you do not need a path (which in itself will make the area feel more spacious) and plants can be grown in pots or planted into the soil beneath the gravel. An advantage of using pots is that they give the gardener the opportunity of altering the balance of the garden from time to time, so that interest is maintained. To begin with, an acer in a large pot might be placed fairly close to the house, with a collection of shrubs in smaller pots in the second section, and even smaller ones placed amongst some attractive rocks against the end wall. The overall effect will be to elongate the area and provide a depth of field.

To create an altogether different perspective, you could place the largest shrub two thirds of the way down the garden, and the medium-sized plants near the building, with the smallest shrubs at the end. The area between the building and the largest shrub would feel smaller, while the area between the large shrub and the

smallest plant would still retain a certain sense of distance.

Alternatively, to foreshorten the garden, you could arrange the plants in the traditional Western way, and put the largest one against the end wall, the medium-sized ones in the middle section, and arrange the smallest plants close to the building. This arrangement effectively draws the end of the garden towards the building.

Vertical features are important in a planting scheme because they link the ground to the sky above and provide a sense of scale. They bring a three-dimensional feel to a design, which makes the garden seem more comfortable and better balanced. Even the most windswept garden needs at least one plant that is taller and more distinctive than its neighbours. In cool climates most plants have reduced growth in windy sites and only some will grow at all. In such conditions, a tough shrub, such as one of the many hawthorns (*Crataegus*) or an arbutus, would be ideal. In warmer areas on the other hand, a small pine, like the Mountain pine (*Pinus mugo*), would bring a welcome touch of green to the site all year round.

Horizontal features are necessary in order to create a feeling of space. There are some plants that grow into a naturally broad shape; *Viburnum plicatum* 'Rowallane' has nicely layered horizontal branches, as do some of the junipers. Horizontal emphasis can also be devised by creating a massed planting of just one type of plant, so as to form a strong broad shape. In this way, even plants with few distinguishing features take on a sculptural quality.

MASSING AND SCULPTING

As garden design becomes ever more individual and representative of the owner, gardeners are becoming increasingly adventurous in ways of using quite ordinary plants. Massing one type of plant to create a defined shape can bring enormous strength and clarity to a plot.

Using just one type of plant repeatedly has the effect of emphasizing its qualities so that they have the greatest impact. Understanding the plant's dominant qualities is therefore essential to achieve the design goals the gardener specifically has in mind. The better the understanding of a plant's attributes, the more sophisticated and cohesive the planting plan can be.

In the hilly landscape of California, deep swathes of lavender soften the contours of rocky gardens, thereby bringing a feeling of order and peace to a wild landscape. The gentleness

of the mass planting of lavender is emphasized still further when edged with a contrasting deep border composed of the blue-green sword-shaped leaves of bearded iris, which grow erect from ground-hugging rhizomes.

Californian gardeners appear to see planting *en masse* as a way of creating a highly evocative space. They use plants like the threads in an embroidery picture: singly they have no meaning, but combined they produce a living textural picture that is highly architectural and complements the nearby buildings.

For a powerful and more tropical effect,

Above: The textural qualities of the four plant elements in this garden have been used to maximum effect by placing them in horizontal lines. The darkness of the wood makes the perfect background to the two varieties of mass-planted grasses. These are balanced by a foreground of smooth emerald-green grass. Sunlight illuminates the flowering miscanthus, bringing it alive and so emphasizing the deep darkness behind and the vibrancy of the lawn in front.

palms and cycas can be planted thickly together. They need good quality soil, moisture and, when young, at least partial shade. As their overall size and shape can be predicted, they are ideal for restricted areas. The Japanese sago palm (*Cycas revoluta*) is tougher than many palms and is wonderfully decorative. It throws out masses of shiny, often dark green, feathery fronds from a central point creating an impression of spreading, rounded gentleness. This can be used to soften the hard contours of nearby buildings whilst adding interest and style.

In cool climates, big cities are sometimes warm enough to make it is possible to achieve a certain type of tropical garden. Mass-planting Tasmanian tree ferns

Above: Mass planting of Golden barrel cacti (*Echinocactus grusonii*) around a tall trichocereus has created a textural design that is modern and humorous. The light catches the plants' spines and makes them glow in the same way that the silk threads catch the light in a tapestry.

(*Dicksonia antarctica*) is one way of doing this. Other trees of varying height can be retained, or placed, around the perimeters, successfully hiding the surrounding buildings. The higher canopies of the trees would help keep any rogue frosts off the tree ferns below, and in summer they would enhance the jungle-like atmosphere of the plot.

In a small garden, it is harder to create this jungle-like feel, but an area can be totally transformed for a few months in the summer by planting the fast-growing perennial Elecampane (*Inula helenium*). A perennial from central Asia, it has a tall erect stem topped with yellow daisy-type flowers. Its

Opposite: The green of a tropical garden is broken by a clump of *Dracaena marginata* 'Tricolor'. Its delicate, spiky leaves contrast well with nearby foliage and that of the palm. Using one type of plant only to carpet the ground anchors the planting scheme and helps to reveal the full design potential of the plants themselves.

leaves are magnificent, being paddle-shaped with a slightly silvery underside; the lower ones can be up to 1m (3ft) long, and winter-flowering primulas seem quite happy to spend the summer under their shade. They will add a really lush feel to a shady corner.

A whole clump of elecampane planted in a flowering meadow garden will make a striking impact, its huge sculptural leaves contrasting effectively with the flower-strewn grass. Further interest can be created by also planting the tall grey-leafed thistle (*Onopordum nervosum*), at precise regular intervals. This will make a three-dimensional picture, with the grass providing a horizontal

Above: This garden has been given a strong personality by using a few key plants in a well thought-out way. Gentle mounds of lavender planted thickly in the foreground continue down the edge of the pathway beyond, linking the two areas together. This brings a feeling of calmness to the area that is delightfully restful.

contast to the vertical lines of the thistles.

Even the humble cabbage can be used as a designer plant. In the kitchen gardens of Villandry, France, low box hedges hold an infill geometric planting of cabbages, leeks and ruby chard. The cabbages are chosen for their solid form and winter colour, which become even more alluring when the leaves are rimmed with frost. The horizontal yet architectural planting creates a strong visual counterpoint to the impressive buildings of the château behind.

Generally, the concept of using a great many of the same sculptural plants is worth copying, even on a small scale, as it achieves a clarity of design that creates an harmonious, and at the same time stylish, atmosphere in the garden.

Left: The unfurling new leaves of the dogwood (*Cornus alternifolia* 'Argentea') reveal the naturally tiered shape of this beautiful small tree. The mass planting of forget-me-nots (*Myosotis*) beneath it make a solid block of colour that complements the airiness of the dogwood.

Above: A simple but cleverly considered planting of grasses has been made more dynamic with the addition of a handsome sword-leafed phormium and a large clump of *Sedum* 'Autumn Joy', resplendent in its winter colour. The back-drop of conifers has the effect of heightening the russet and fawn shades of the grasses and emphasizing their delicate feathery seed-heads.

Above: Cabbages and spinach planted thickly in low squares become beautiful and textural. The blue-mauve rounded cabbage leaves contrast handsomely with those of the fresh green spinach, proving that considered plant combinations can increase the overall impact of the scheme.

PLANTS FOR PONDS AND STREAMS

The smallest of ponds adds depth of interest to a garden, making it feel more balanced and more in harmony with the natural world. Designer plants placed around a pool perimeter, or planted in the pool itself, give it a personality and transform it into an object of sheer beauty and delight. As the giver of life, water is a key element, and the planting should reinforce this. It is a design concept which was clearly expressed by the Impressionist painter Monet in his water garden at Giverny, France. By breaking up the wide expanse of water with large floating clumps of water lilies, he further enhanced the beauty and importance of the pond.

Above: The bold leaves and flowers of *Lysichiton camtschatcensis* contrast well with the lax sword-shaped leaves of the irises behind and the delicate yellow flowers of *Primula prolifera*. The different leaf shapes combine to make an exciting and arresting bog planting.

Before choosing any plants it is best to analyze the general situation. Is there earth around the pond and, if so, is it permanently damp so that bog plants may be grown? Or is there paving up to the edges, making it necessary to use containers for plants? Does the pond or stream have sloping sides or a shallow shelf, so that marginal plants which prefer their heads out of water and their feet well in it can be grown? Finally, how deep is the pond? This will determine which water lilies can be chosen, as some need a greater depth of water than others.

Informal gardens benefit enormously

from having a pond of some sort to create a relaxed atmosphere. If a pond has straight sides, and appears too formal and rigid, a wise choice of planting, hanging slightly over its edges, can soften the overall design. Small shrubs such as Woolly willow (*Salix lanata*), cistus or *Salvia officinalis* can be pruned to gently bend over the water. Choose plants that do not frequently shed dead leaves and flowers into the water. Perennials such as Lady's mantle (*Alchemilla mollis*) look appropriately relaxed beside the water but flowerheads should be removed before they begin to decay. If

Above: Allowing marginal plants to encroach over its edges has softened the formality of this oblong pond. The distinctive lance-shaped leaves of pontederia harmonize with the container-planted hosta nearby while the smooth, round water lily leaves balance the long narrow leaves of the irises and variegated grass that are planted at the back of the pond.

Above: The outline of this natural-looking pond has been completely obscured by planting marginal irises and Monkey musk (*Mimulus*) right up to its edges, and by placing *Alchemilla mollis*, astilbes, sedums and cotoneaster to overhang the water. In this way, the pond has become an interactive part of the overall planting of the garden.

paving surrounds the pond, one or two flagstones can easily be lifted to create planting pockets for proud clumps of the Royal fern (*Osmunda regalis*) or the ethereal angels' fishing rods (*Dierama*). The latter are tall, relaxed and elegant in style; their arching stems carry nodding, pink bell-shaped flowers and fit into an informal garden admirably.

If a pool has an irregular shape and has been positioned with flowerbeds close by, the choice of planting is much greater. A marginal plant with distinctive lance-shaped leaves is the blue-flowered Pickerel weed, (*Pontederia cordata*). Its leaves contrast effectively with the floating perennial Water soldier (*Stratiotes aloides*), that has rosettes of razor-sharp, sword-shaped leaves. Grown in

abundance, this plant gives a pond a very stylish look.

A bog garden can sometimes need some extra definition, being neither water nor flowerbed; this can be achieved by adding some designer plants to the overall design. In cool climates one of the best choices is the Yellow skunk cabbage (*Lysichiton americanus*), which, planted *en masse*, creates a stunning picture in spring, when its bright yellow spathes (a bract protecting the flower within) appear before its large shiny green leaves. This exotic plant also looks at home in a jungle garden, next to luxuriant large-leafed plants. *Gunnera manicata* is one of the most flamboyant plants for the water's edge. It resembles rhubarb, and its leaves can reach more than 1.5 m (5ft) across. Ligularia, with its large fleshy leaves on slim stems, also adds a lush tropical feel to any garden, especially when planted next to *Darmera peltata*, which has large, round, scalloped-edged leaves.

In tropical climates the garden owner has an exciting range of large-leafed plants to choose from for poolside planting. Their impact is doubled when they are reflected in a limpid pool. Palms and banana plants growing amongst clumps of the huge arrow-shaped leaves of *Xanthosoma sagittifolium* give an aura of primeval forest as they cast deep shadows over the water's surface. *Cordyline fruticosa*, with its long, variegated, slender leaves, emphasizes the leaves of the *Xanthosoma* and the Japanese banana plant (*Musa basjoo*), while adding elegance to the planting. In the truly tropical pond, *Lotus amazonica* can be grown to bring a touch of the East to the plot.

Cool courtyard gardens with the simplest of ponds can be set off by a single water lily. The flat round leaves act as a counterbalance to the straight lines of the walls and soften the whole area. Height can be provided by planting a clump of a sedge such as Umbrella grass (*Cyperus involucratus*) at the pond margin: it has decorative green umbels on long stems that gently rustle in the breeze.

DESIGNING WITH TEXTURE

As a gardener becomes more adept at placing key plants so that they punctuate the plot and draw the eye to specific areas, he or she will also notice that the overall impact is in some ways dependent on the juxtaposition of different textures. The ideal planting plan takes these considerations into account, and includes plants that vary in their light-reflective and textural qualities.

Shiny-leafed plants reflect the light, and because of this they can be dazzling on sunny days. In exposed gardens, where light intensity levels are high, such plants often look their best amongst others whose leaves absorb the light. *Acanthus mollis*, for example, planted in large swathes, loses much of its design appeal, as the leaves reflect too much light, confusing the eye. On the other hand, when interspersed with grey-leafed santolina, or with lavender, its architectural qualities are clearly set off and immediately have more impact.

It is perfectly possible to design a garden that has great depth of interest using only different foliage plants. Leaf textures are as wide-ranging as leaf shapes and together various leaves can form endless combinations. For example, some forms of rhododendron, such as *Rhododendron* subsp. *fictolacteum*, have a matt green upper-leaf surface but a wonderfully woolly rust-coloured under-surface.

When choosing companion plants, take note of the texture of their leaves. Is it smooth and glossy, such as that of musa, smooth and matt, such as that of ligularia, felted as in lavender and santolina, or woolly, as in *Verbascum olympicum*? Mix and match plant leaves in the same way that you might for interior soft furnishings.

Grey leaves are often rough, and this drastically reduces their light-reflective qualities. *Verbascum bombyciferum*, *Onopordon acanthium* and *Cynara cardunculus* all have large leaves that, even on the sunniest of days, reflect very little

light. This makes them ideal for sunny gardens as they actually reduce the amount of glare from the sun, making the whole scene easier on the eye.

In shady plots, large shiny leaves come into their own. Small amounts of light, filtering through overhead trees or between tall buildings, are caught and thrown back into the garden. A dull and gloomy corner can thus easily be enlivened by growing a shrub or perennial that has the ability to glow in the shade.

Above: Two key plants have been used in this garden to create a highly textural yet romantic and gentle scene. The ripe seed-heads of the grass *Hordeum jubatum* flutter among clumps of *Iris sibirica* leaves in the low autumn sunshine.

Opposite: Colour can accentuate and emphasize the character of a choice plant. Here, the clear apple green of the canna leaf is reinforced by its companion plant, *Perilla frutescens*. The deep-maroon crinkled leaves of the perilla set off the smooth clear lines of the canna to perfection.

DESIGNING WITH COLOUR

The fact that few people would photograph a garden in black and white demonstrates the power of colour. Different colours act on our subconscious, making us feel relaxed or alert. Japanese gardens, for example, rely heavily on a variety of green foliage, and use colour very sparingly: this makes them unusually tranquil spaces in which to sit or walk. When they do grow a flowering plant or use vibrant colour, its impact can be similar to that of dropping a pebble into a still pool. When you see clipped waves of vibrant pink azaleas pulsating among neat pines, it provokes a strong emotional response.

Above: The bright, sculptural, orange-red flowerheads of red-hot pokers (*Kniphofia rooperi*), which turn orange-yellow in late autumn, provide a welcome splash of colour in flowerbeds, at a time of year when most other herbaceous perennials are dying down.

A plant that has no distinctive leaf or flower can be used in a sculptural way if it is planted in blocks or rows. A cottage garden in early spring will have little colour and form, as the summer-flowering perennials have yet to grow, but it can gain definition by planting single-coloured tulips in clumps and surrounding them with masses of sky-blue forget-me-nots. Planted singly the latter have little design impact, but if allowed to seed freely they will cover any bare earth, providing a blue background to any flowering bulbs that rise above them.

To get the most benefit from colour, it is important to use plants with the same colour intensity or strength. Large grey-leafed plants are ideal placed amongst the pastel colours of a cottage garden. Their size and style allows them to stand out, but their tonal values are similar, creating a more harmonious picture.

A garden that has many dark-leafed plants, such as junipers, hollies, laurel and pines, has the strength of character not to be overwhelmed by scarlet poppies, orange day lilies (*Hemerocallis*) or brilliantly yellow *Rudbeckia fulgida*. Too many 'heavy' greens can be oppressive, and planting large architectural grey-leafed plants singly, or mass-planting small grey-leafed plants, such as santolina and lavender, can rectify this.

Colour can be used to make a dramatic statement or to gently draw attention to a gem of a plant growing discreetly close by. It is the gardener's job to decide which response to evoke.

Contemporary buildings are often painted in strong colours that emphasize their planes and angles. Their surroundings therefore benefit from equally strong sculptural plants that have a good solid colour: dark green, maroon and grey foliage looks striking against blue or terracotta walls, and if the plants have a distinctive shape as well, so much the better.

Above: The stately shape and style of the glowing *Eryngium giganteum* is in sharp contrast to the onion seed-heads that rise above low-growing leaves. In the background deeply-cut vine leaves accentuate the glossy foliage of the bay tree growing nearby and of the neatly clipped box edging.

DESIGNING WITH FORM

When planting is of a uniform colour, shape becomes all-important, as it adds visual variety to the garden. In a wild garden, where green is the dominant colour, depth of interest will be added by well-shaped perennials or shrubs. A meadow instantly becomes more appealing when a handsome Giant fennel (*Ferula communis*) or angelica (*Angelica archangelica officinalis*) towers majestically above the waving grass.

With a good understanding of the importance of light, texture, colour and form, a gardener can create a spell-binding haven, delightful at all times. At the planning stage a decision has to be made as to how he or she wants the garden to be viewed. If there is a wonderful view from a particular area, plants can be positioned so as to lead the eye to it. This is especially important when there is an eyesore just beyond the plot's boundary. By channelling and guiding the eye to the best aspect, neighbouring ugly areas can become less noticeable.

Placing plants of varying shapes in a garden creates a tension that gives the plot energy. The level of this energy depends on the form of the plants chosen and how they are mixed and matched. Placing contrasting forms together heightens tension, in the same way that boulders draw attention to surrounding smooth water.

A plot that is entirely composed of large topiary shapes has an intense energy that is enjoyable in small doses but which is not conducive to lengthy contemplation. At the opposite end of the scale, a grass meadow with no contrasting forms is so relaxing it can induce visitors to forget time completely. Ideally, the gardener should aim to create a garden that is both energizing and restful, by placing large-leafed plants and shrubs with a distinct form among small-leafed ones.

3
Hiding and Disguising Eyesores

INCREASING URBANIZATION HAS RESULTED in people living in much closer proximity to each other; as a result, most city dwellers long for a private and secluded spot where they can briefly escape the pressures of urban life. If they are lucky enough to have a garden, a courtyard or a roof terrace, it is well within their power to create a world of their own into which they can retreat in one quick moment.

Privacy can be obtained by screening immediate neighbouring buildings that overpower and dominate. Even if it is not possible to hide them entirely, their impact can be mimimized visually by breaking up their outline. Trees, shrubs, climbers and large perennials can be used to perform this task admirably, and if they have a positive shape and style – in other words, if they are designer plants – further strength of purpose will be achieved. This will detract even more from exterior influences, as they will act as the picture frame to the garden within. Even within a garden there may be immovable structures that are unsightly and which one would prefer to disguise. Sheds and small brick storerooms usually have little architectural merit and are often improved by being masked by some beautiful sculptural plants or by vigorous climbers.

Left: This terraced city garden is effectively screened from the nearby buildings with layers of tall foliage plants so that views can be glimpsed through from one area to the other and a feeling of airiness is retained. Yellow-flowered ligularia, plummy-leafed acer and coral-flowered macleaya generate a feeling of lushness in the secluded seating area.

BOUNDARY PLANTS

If your garden is surrounded either by buildings or a landscape that do not blend with the style of garden you have planned, boundary shrubs and trees should be used to disguise them and distract the eye. A tall clipped hedge of yew or hornbeam with neat box parterres and tall Italian cypress (*Cypressus sempervirens*) would be a good choice for a formal Italianate garden. Space allowing, a selection of native medium-sized trees and shrubs could be grown instead of a hedge, effecting a startling contrast with the dark green of the cypresses. If a denser perimeter planting is needed, then various pines, such as the quick-growing Loblolly pine (*Pinus taeda*) or Austrian pine (*Pinus nigra*) would look attractive, especially if deciduous vase-shaped trees were planted at intervals amongst them.

Opposite: A dark, solid yew hedge shuts out the world beyond this garden, making it feel secure and secret. The tall yew provides the perfect background for a loosely-growing delicate white rose, mauve alliums, grey santolina, plum-coloured *Salvia officinalis* 'Purpurascens' and lilac-coloured violas.

An informal cottage garden requires a framework of mainly mixed deciduous trees and shrubs to complement the predominantly relaxed planting style, but it also needs structural elements to give it a better defined appearance. These can be introduced very effectively in perimeter planting. Traditionally, holly (*Ilex*) was chosen for hedging in this type of garden, partly because it was believed to have protective qualities, mainly against evil and against lightning. Mountain ash (*Sorbus aucuparia*), a decorative, rounded-to-conical tree, was planted for the same reason. A large, neatly shaped shrub that also suits the character of a cottage garden is *Pittosporum* 'Garnettii'; with its soft evergreen leaves edged with silver, it never dominates the more small-flowered species so often grown in this type of garden. Many of the mahonias, with their decorative shiny evergreen leaves, are perfectly happy to grow in the light shade of boundary trees and shrubs, and look equally handsome beside an unsightly shed. Always bear in mind that perimeter planting feels more natural and interesting when tall trees and shrubs are under-planted with well-shaped medium- and small-sized shrubs.

Gardens that are a bit more structured than cottage gardens can accommodate perimeter plants with a more sophisticated personality. Portugal laurel (*Prunus lusitanica*) and Cherry laurel (*Prunus laurocerasus*) are attractive evergreen shrubs that help to create a solid boundary year round; fairly large shrubs, when allowed to grow to their natural shape and size, which is solid and well-defined, they also make good wind breaks.

Small to medium evergreen shrubs are invaluable where a boundary needs only to be partially screened. Mexican orange blossom (*Choisya ternata*) has glossy leaves arranged in whorls of three leaflets and makes a tidy compact shape that looks good at the back of a border. *Fatsia japonica* is another distinctive evergreen that introduces a sense of style to the dullest corner; it has large hand-shaped lobed leaves that resemble a fig leaf, and looks equally at home in a jungle style garden as in formally landscaped settings.

The more individual a garden is the more important it is to disguise and screen out anything which does not enhance its personality. The Queensland umbrella tree (*Schefflera actinophylla*) makes an ideal barrier against wind and unpleasant views in warm, urban, subtropical gardens. It is a very

decorative tree, with wonderful, glossy, thick-rounded and divided leaves which are held in an umbrella fashion. Its architectural merits become more apparent when it is grown near the New Zealand puka (*Meryta sinclairi*) which has a dense head of large dark shiny leaves that point upwards and outwards. Both plants sit well with palms and cordylines.

Cool climate seaside gardens are the hardest of all to screen in a stylish way, as the vast majority of plants that can tolerate salt-laden winds often have tiny leaves. *Griselinia littoralis* is invaluable in these situations. It can withstand exposure in seaside locations, and its distinctive, well-rounded, leathery green leaves look very fine when grown, for example, near the feather-leafed tamarisk (*Tamarix*), which resembles billowing pink clouds when in flower.

Left: This simple boundary fence has almost been lost among a profusion of plants. Tall angelica, with its green flower umbels, conifers, ivy and evergreen *Euphoria mellifera* carry the eye up and over the fence to the trees and hills beyond the garden. With so much of interest to look at, the fence becomes the least important element in the scene.

CLIMBERS AND WALL SHRUBS

Climbers and wall shrubs are invaluable plants in any situation, but they are essential in town gardens, or in any small garden where vertical features are necessary to help create an illusion of space. With the right choice of plant, walls, dividers and buildings can be made to look attractive, and can be incorporated into the overall design of the garden.

Above: The well-shaped leaves of Golden hop (*Humulus lupulus 'Aureus'*) add a highly decorative touch to this wall and at the same time camouflage it very successfully. The vivid yellow-green of the hop brings out the colour of the purple flowers of *Solanum crispum* 'Glasnevin'.

Right: A modern red-brick wall has been turned into a breathtaking object of beauty by training wisteria over its entire height and width. Bearded irises hide the base of the wall and harmonize with it, emphasizing the delicate wisteria flowers.

Climbers are plants that have an urge to grow upwards, and sometimes sideways, in their quest to reach the sky. They do this by various means. Some produce tiny suckers, which cling on tenaciously to their host (ivies, for example), making the need for tying them to a fixed support unnecessary. Such plants are well worth growing where the expanse of wall is so large it is not practical to attach wire supports or a wooden trellis to it. However, they do wander where they will over their host, and are only kept in check by the wind or by severe pruning. Given the choice, most would rather not climb over a wall to face the prevailing winds but prefer to stay on the more sheltered side. *Hydrangea petiolaris* is a good example of this kind of climber. Ideal for hiding a really ugly wall, it has suckers that securely attach themselves to brick, and requires no further help to do its job. Its leaves are well shaped, and the flowerheads are highly decorative: large, lacy and white when in full bloom, they turn an ornamental russet brown when they die, which looks very attractive in winter, when covered in hoar-frost or snow.

Another type of climber (grape vines, for example) produces tendrils that resemble small springs. These reach towards a support and then tighten themselves around it, thereby securely attaching the whole plant to the support. Their growth can be slightly wayward, but can be directed by tying new shoots onto wires pointing in the direction in which you want them to grow. To cover a large expanse of boundary wall or fencing, grow the vigorous, large-leafed Japanese crimson glory vine, *Vitis coignetiae*. Its tendrils are not enough to completely support it, but it will happily scramble through and over support wires and will provide stunning autumn colour.

The third kind of climber can actually wrap itself around a thin support. This type will happily travel along any wire or pole and therefore can be used for making living designs on a blank wall. Most clematis and

Above: The shape of this serpentine wall has been enhanced with a series of espalier fruit trees. The neatly trained lateral branches produce a mass of flowers that will successfully fruit against the warmth of the wall. Together, the wall and the fruit trees make a decorative barrier against the outside world.

honeysuckles fall in this category. Clematis are usually grown solely for their flowers, but *Clematis armandii* has large oval evergreen to semi-evergreen leaflets that are very stylish. Like many clematis, it prefers to have its feet in the shade and its head and shoulders in the light. This makes it an ideal candidate for the back of a border, where its distinctive leaves and pale pink flowers can be seen to perfection. The most decorative of the evergreen honeysuckles is *Lonicera japonica henryii*, whose long and spear-shaped leaves provide winter interest. Another twining perennial climber that makes a strong statement is Golden hop (*Humulus lupulus* 'Aureus'); its vivid golden green leaves are vine-shaped and look stunning against either the dark wood of a shed or covering an archway. A woody climber that should be grown more often, not only for its apple green leaves that are composed of five oval

leaflets on a simple stalk, but also for its deliciously chocolate–scented flowers, is *Akebia quinata*. It can develop into an unruly mass if not checked, but its leaves look very pretty covering the tiled roof of a barn or clothing the branches of a host tree.

Lastly, there are climbers that have the desire to spread themselves but have to be pruned and tied to their support in order to thrive and look attractive (climbing roses, for example). If the garden is already surrounded by a wooden fence or by a wall, Japanese wineberry (*Rubus phoenicolasius*) can be grown against it to display its attractive bramble-like leaves and russet-coloured stems to their best advantage.

Wall shrubs, though not climbers, are woody plants which have no objection to having a solid surface right behind them. Many, in fact, prefer the warmth and protection from strong winds that a wall gives

Left: The uniformity of a plain brick wall has been transformed with ivy grown over diamond shapes that reflect those in the tiled roof above. A low box hedge disguises the flowerbed at the base of the wall and also completes the design, giving it tremendous style.

Above: *Hydrangea petiolaris* has spread itself around and over a collection of unsightly drain pipes; older plants sport decorative dried flowerheads in winter, and so are valuable all year. A variegated evergreen ivy has been planted as a companion to the hydrangea and will, in time, help to disguise the ugly pipe work. Both plants complement the smooth roundness of the stone wall to which they cling.

them. Some even benefit from being tied in here and there to a wall, so that winds cannot get behind them, tip them forwards and unbalance them. The evergreen *Magnolia grandiflora* tree, with wonderfully thick, shiny leaves and large creamy white flowers, will tolerate alkaline soil, although it prefers acid soil. It always looks magnificent growing against a tall wall. In northern climates this can have the added benefit of giving it wind-chill protection, so it is ideally suited for camouflaging a boring wall.

Where a boundary needs only to be gently screened, tall-growing perennials are ideal, as they interrupt the view beyond without totally obscuring it. The wonderfully plummy *Angelica gigas*, which grows as tall as a man, brings a distinctive air to any plot with its majestic character. Alternatively, the same effect could be achieved by a row of Oak-leaved hydrangea (*Hydrangea*

quercifolia) which has marvellously sculptural, coloured leaves in autumn.

In warm climates the Japanese mock orange (*Pittosporum tobira*), with thick, dark, evergreen leaves attractively arranged on numerous branching stems, makes a good screening plant. In a courtyard garden, a container-grown Tree of heaven (*Ailanthus altissima*) can bring interest, height and shade, and can also be used to hide any unsightly building there may be beyond the confines of the courtyard. It has very stylish leaves that open reddish-tinged before fading to green. Owing to its vigorous suckering growth, it is better grown in a container than in a flowerbed, where it can run wild.

Grasses in general bring movement and sound to a garden. As they have flexible stems (or culms), they introduce a relaxed and mellow mood, something that is becoming increasingly valuable in these frenetic times.

PLANTS TO DISTRACT

Not all architectural plants are woody or solid in growth. Many grasses (and they include bamboo, sedges, rushes and reedmaces) grow into thick clumps that have a distinctive, albeit gentle, silhouette for much of their growing season. Late-flowering grasses are invaluable for the autumn and winter gardens when other perennials are past their best.

Left: A late autumn garden need not be devoid of interest. Here, the different shapes and textures draw attention away from the unattractive structure behind. Conical-shaped conifers take the eye on a journey amongst the plume-like heads of miscanthus which catch the sunlight and contrast with the stout brown seed-heads of the teasel (*Dipsacus fullonum*).

Their rounded outlines act as a perfect foil to clipped hedges and topiary and, planted *en masse*, create a sense of space and distance. This is because their simple, subtly-coloured shape allows the eye to float over the scenery, making an area appear larger than it actually is.

Moving with the gentlest of breezes, grasses send a whisper through the garden that is reminiscent of waves gently lapping the shoreline on a summer's day – a deeply refreshing sound to the spirit. Where a garden faces east to west, grasses are one of the best architectural plants to grow, as their seed-heads catch both the morning and evening light, looking radiantly beautiful.

Tall grasses such as *Miscanthus sinsensis* 'Flamingo', which is warmly coloured in autumn, or *Stipa gigantea*, with its handsome golden-seeded panicles, provide magical

focal points when planted amongst shorter-growing perennials. Grasses that retain their seed-heads well into winter, *Cortaderia selloana* and *Miscanthus sinensis* 'Kaskade', are invaluable for providing structural elements in bare periods. Snow and heavy hoar-frosts only heighten their beauty by emphasizing their mop of panicles standing proudly above other perennial seed-heads.

In exposed sites grasses can prove to be invaluable for adding height and character. Their flexible stems are well able to withstand winds that would flatten other less sturdy plants. Wind-swept plots are drier than more sheltered sites, and there are many grasses, such as *Molina caerulea* ssp. *Arundunacea* 'Transparent' and Switch grass (*Panicum virgatum*), or Blue fescue grass (*Festuca glauca*) that thrive in very dry conditions. These plants look marvellous grown amongst more rigid neighbours such as *Crambe maritima*, with its thick blue-grey crinkly leaves.

In a minimalist garden of gravel and rocks, a thick planting of the golden Hakone grass (*Hakonechloa macra* 'Alboaurea') makes a powerful impact. It seems to know that its lemon yellow and green striped leaves look stunning when they fall in the same direction to make a thick mound, and obligingly performs.

America is the home of many varieties of corn (*Zea*), and there are now many beautiful forms coming onto the market that are grown for their foliage, coloured stems or distinctive tasselled seed-heads. In countries where summers are less consistently hot, the tassel-headed *Zea* 'Hungarian Red' is invaluable for adding height in the autumn plot when many other perennials have died back. It has the further advantage of springing upright after a drenching or a gale.

Bamboos bring a strong Oriental element to a garden. There is a bamboo to suit any situation: they can be either short or very tall, and all of those in cultivation are evergreen, making them ideal for small gardens where every plant has to offer all-round value. Bamboos are either clump-forming or spreading and gardeners with limited space should choose the former variety as the spreading ones can quickly become invasive. Some bamboos are selected for their variegated leaves, others for their decorative stems. Many are suited to being grown in containers, although as hungry feeders they will need regular feeding. Container-grown plants are more vulnerable to the cold and heat, so hardiness is a consideration. Grown in pots, they look very effective when massed together at the end of a decking platform, where the sound of their rustling leaves can reach nearby rooms.

Very small gardens can be made mysterious and atmospheric by planting large

Opposite: Grasses look particularly fine when placed together and have the advantage of making a 'complete' picture that will last into the winter and look even more dramatic when covered in a delicate coating of frost.

Above: The distinctively shaped leaves of veratrum draw attention to the variegated slender leaves of the grass *Hakonechloa macra* 'Aureola'. In turn, they make a perfect background to the veratrum's heavily pleated oval leaves.

Below: A varied collection of bamboo and grasses grown in posts and placed at different heights disguise the corner of this city garden. Even the slightest breeze will cause them to shimmer and move, and their movement brings repeated interest to the area. Their visual impact can be altered from time to time by simply repositioning the pots.

towering clumps of different bamboos to form a thicket opening out into a small glade which houses a simple bench. In a confined space the colour of the clumps and the way the leaves are arranged is very noticeable, and therefore careful thought should go into their choice. Since the bamboo remains verdant the plot will be beautiful all year round.

A mixed perennial border will become more exciting if tall plants partially obscure the view beyond them. If the border is very colourful, a block of green or a suitably muted colour will introduce a feeling of stability and strength to the planting design. The willow-leaved sunflower (*Helianthus salicifolius*), which grows to 2.5m (8ft) and has delicate lance-shaped leaves, is clump-forming, with an airy but positive character. Grown for its delicate foliage rather than for its flowers, it adds enough height to gently break the line of

vision, thereby giving a plot greater general sense of dimension.

A beautiful evergreen shrub that is worth growing either in a flower border or beside a hedge is Honey spurge (*Euphorbia mellifera*). It has a tall rounded shape, attractive lance-shaped leaves and honey-scented flowers. All these qualities make it particularly valuable in the smaller garden, where its height and bulk can be used to achieve a sense of scale.

Where there are mainly small shrubs, you should consider breaking up the line of vision

at various points with perennials that have a graceful but distinctive personality. The Giant lily (*Cardiocrinum giganteum*) has an upright stem with beautiful scented white flowers that would provide a vertical counterpoint to many low-growing shrubs. An alternative could be echinops, which produces globular blue flowerheads on tall stems, lasting well into autumn, above well-shaped dark-green leaves. It is an ideal foil for setting off lighter coloured plants, and at the same time not detracting attention from them.

Above: A deeply planted border has been given key focal points to distract and lead the eye through the planting. Blue-green sword-like leaves of Bearded iris at the front of the border are picked up in the centre by a fine *Melianthus major* of the same colour; close by the magenta flowerheads of cynara carry the eye on and up to the nearby rose and honeysuckle.

ENHANCING LOW-GROWING PLANTINGS

When planning a garden, consider how well the plants are put together at ground level, not just at waist and head height. This is especially important around seating areas. The eye should be able to travel high and low, finding dynamic plant combinations that give pleasure and interest, and discovering delightful groups of plants tucked down low in corners or beneath taller plants. Good ground-hugging combinations have an endearing quality that should not be underestimated: they enrich the whole garden (especially for small children, who notice them more than adults do, and who are the world's future gardeners!)

Above right: Heat-loving, low-growing plants thrive in a gravel garden where the drainage is good, provided there is ample light. Tall Bearded iris leaves link the dianthus and the poppies to the denser planting that surrounds this hot area, where a bronze-leafed phormium and variegated agave add dynamic focal points.

Many low-growing plants can be grown in cottage gardens, and in order to give their grouping cohesion, some of them at least should be structural. One such plant, that is currently underused and easily grown from seed, is *Plantago major* var. *atropurpurea*. It is similar to the common plantain, but has deep maroon-coloured, club-shaped leaves like those of hostas. Its unusual foliage looks particularly good amongst the grey spiky leaves of pinks (*Dianthus*), as the leaf-shape of the former emphasizes that of the latter. Dianthus itself can be made to look distinctive, by planting an old-fashioned single-flowering variety thickly beneath a standard tree and after flowering keeping the clump trimmed so that the plants resemble a thick grey carpet.

Stachys byzantina is another ground-hugging, evergreen perennial with soft grey leaves which has a structural effect when grown *en masse* and kept neatly trimmed. It makes an excellent edging plant at the front of a border and adds style when planted thickly around the base of an urn or other garden ornaments.

In the cottage and woodland garden, thick plantings of lungwort (*Pulmonaria*) can be interspersed with *Euphorbia griffithii*, which has scarlet flowerheads. Some pulmonarias have quite rounded leaves, whilst others have long narrow ones; some are heavily spotted with silver, others are almost entirely silver-coloured. Although their spring flowers are attractive, their main value lies in their distinctive foliage.

Another architectural clump-forming choice for a shaded area is *Epimedium* x *rubrum*. It provides good ground cover and looks delightful growing around the base of a tree

trunk or at the foot of a wall. *Cyclamen hederifolium*, an autumn-flowering plant from the Mediterranean, also likes to grow in the light shade of a tree. After flowering, its heart-shaped, silver-mottled leaves are held in tight, well-formed clumps for the entire winter. It looks most attractive at the base of a yew hedge, where its leaves form a striking contrast with the yew above. *Hacquetia epipactis* is a tiny plant that makes neat clumps in woodland gardens. Its late-winter yellow flowers resemble a miniature golden ball, supported by a circle of rounded apple-green bracts.

The area under some trees can be so shaded and dry that only ivy will grow. There are many ivies that are quite stylish, with widely differing leaf shapes and colours. Three strongly varying types in shaped blocks or patterns will create an exciting, living evergreen textural rug.

Left: A coastal garden has been given great style with the addition of a variegated *Agave americana*. Its strong shape and positive colour adds a feeling of permanence to the simple planting of helianthemum which scrambles through well-placed sea urchins. The smooth roundness of the urchins accentuates the length and sharpness of the agave leaves.

Left: Low-growing plants become visually more powerful when they are planted simply in blocks of colour. In this scheme, mauve violas thread their way among purple spikes of veronica and the dainty flowers of gypsophila. The key plant here is *Ajania pacifica*. Its decorative greyish-white margined leaves add substance to the overall planting, anchoring it to the site.

Above: Discovering a small and unexpected plant in a garden often gives the greatest pleasure. The starburst-shaped evergreen leaves of *Helleborus foetidus* protect the delicate flowers of *Cyclamen hederifolium* as they grow comfortably together in this shaded gravel bed. The cyclamen's small silver-marbled leaves have an endearing charm, tucked beneath those of the more dominant hellebore and they combine to create a perfect picture.

Right: A thick clump of sempervivum clings tenaciously to the mellow clay tiles of a barn roof, drawing attention to their simple quality and beauty. The neat fleshy rosettes, in warm brown tones, harmonize with the tiles so that together they make a discreet but intriguing design.

Elephant's ears (*Bergenia*) are happy growing in light shade, either in cool climates or in sub-tropical conditions. As long as any old leaves are regularly removed, the round fleshy foliage has several decorative qualities. When massed beneath a shrub they can be used to counterbalance the smaller leaves of the shrub above; they also provide positive ground cover. Placed next to a stone, their smooth thick surface can be used to emphasize its rough texture. (This is a design strategy used in Japanese gardens to link an inanimate object with the living ground cover.)

In very hot, dry climates, small succulents have an important role to play in the garden. In fact, gardening with succulents can be highly architectural and abstract, although the success of this type of landscaping is dependent on how the different textures and growth patterns of the various plants are mixed and matched. Many succulents grow in rosettes that are small, neat and compact, while others are very large, with almost grotesque shapes.

Huge plants of agave look dynamic on their own but, when ground-hugging succulents such as aeonium are allowed to scramble amongst them, the whole design becomes even more interesting. In cooler climates, succulents such as house leeks (*Sempervivum*) look attractive growing in the cracks of a wall or a path. Long ago it was common to see a cluster of sempervivum growing decoratively on a tiled roof, proving that in the wrong place, the most wonderfully decorative plant can look ordinary, while, if well-positioned, the smallest plant becomes interesting and stylish.

Above: Here is proof that a 'foliage only' planting can be exciting, interesting and beautiful. In a shady and damp spot, the green-leafed ferns, *Cyrtomium falcatum*, *Dryopteris* 'Stableri' and *Dryopteris wallichiana* mingle with the silver- and purple-leafed fern, *Athyrium niponicum*. The handsomely spotted leaves of *Pulmonaria sacharata* complete the design, making it satisfyingly balanced.

S HAPING EVERGREEN TREES and shrubs allows you great creative freedom, and clipped plants are ideal even in the smallest of gardens. To shape them imaginatively the gardener must take his or her courage in both hands; once that is done, there is no limit to what can be sculpted. It is probably advisable to start with simple shapes cut in box or yew, but as confidence grows more ambitious projects can be embarked upon.

Every garden can be enhanced by the inclusion of at least one or two well-shaped plants; a neat pair of topiary plants in pots will frame a doorway or delineate a path. More ambitiously, plants can be turned into arbours, seats, hedges, wall coverings or contemporary abstract designs. One of the keys to success is to have a clear mental picture of the desired end result. Another is to choose a plant whose growth habit and leaf form is appropriate for the shape to be created. If the shape is to be compact, then box or yew are ideal, because they are both small-leaved, slow-growing and lend themselves to becoming a dense and solid construction. Where a thinner, gentler outline is desired, a small tree or shrub that needs only light trimming is more suitable.

4
Sculpting and Shaping with Plants

Left: Plants can be used in a purely sculptural way and in this Japanese courtyard the potentially montonous brick and gravel has been transformed with the clever inclusion of neatly clipped squares of box. A sophisticated design of this type creates a feeling of serenity and timelessness that is uniquely relaxing and calming.

The general rule is that the more controlled the shape is to be, the slower the plant's growth should be, to avoid having to perpetually snip and trim.

More loosely shaped specimens should give the impression of having a naturally beautiful outline. A small tree with a well-defined trunk and a pleasingly shaped crown adds an understated refinement to the most casual of plots. In confined spaces, espalier and cordon fruit trees have the added advantage of allowing a wider selection of fruit to be harvested than if the trees were left to grow to their natural size, with the added bonus of attractive form and a higher than average yield of fruit, as the fanned out branches get the full benefit of sun and light.

Shaping trees and shrubs can help give a garden a sense of proportion by altering perspective and balance, but careful thought should be given to their positions before planting. A useful tip is to get someone to stand in the proposed position and hold a long pole vertically. This should enable the gardener to envisage how a specimen of similar height but of greater bulk will look and how the dimensions of the plot will be altered by its addition.

Patios and terraces can be enhanced by the addition of one or more attractively sculpted and sized shrubs. In confined spaces they add a sense of permanence as well as introducing a feeling of height and depth by distancing the viewer from the surrounding walls.

Right: Tall pencil slim cypress trees, medium-sized round-headed olive trees and low mounds of lavender have been used as three dominant threads in this garden. They draw the space together around the small pavilion and, in doing so, create a feeling of balance, depth of interest and tranquillity. The dark-leafed cypress trees counterbalance the silver grey leaves of the olive and lavender.

TOPIARY

Topiary is the best-known form of garden sculpture. It is a skill that was well known in Roman times, when cypress was used to create substantial shapes such as ships, and box was used to hedge flowerbeds. The Romans took delight in creating any shape they could imagine, thus introducing a light-hearted touch to their gardens.

The practice then fell into disuse, and medieval gardeners limited their flights of fancy to simple shapes grown over withy frames, but by the end of the 15th century a revival had taken place in Florence, Italy, and plants were once again shaped as animals and buildings. There was such a craze for topiary in the 16th and early 17th century that a wide variety of plants was used, from rosemary and privet to juniper. From the 17th century onwards, parterres were designed using low neat hedges of box to surround coloured earth and gravel, and, later, flowerbeds. As the architecture of nearby buildings became more geometric, so topiary was used to reflect this formality. Evergreen plants such as holly, bay, laurel, *Rhamnus alaternus*, *Phillyrea latifolia* (which has dark green glossy leaves) and, in warmer climates, myrtle, were commonly used.

Above: In this Dutch garden topiary chickens and eggs harmonize with the casual and light-hearted mood of the nearby vegetable and herb garden.

Left: Tall dark yew hedges enclose this geometrically designed topiary garden, making it seem both secretive and unworldly. The neatly clipped dynamic pyramids catch the sun so that light and shade have become an integral element in the overall design.

The fashion declined once again in the second half of the 18th century, and many grand houses did away with their topiary gardens. Only a few examples survived, mostly in cottage gardens, which were often lived in by estate workers who had created the estates' original topiary. By the end of the 19th century, with the rise of the Arts and Crafts movement, this cottage garden topiary flourished once more. At the same time the fashion developed for dense planting of new flowering annuals and perennials in these gardens. This helped to popularize the topiary, as the dark, solid shapes of

peacocks, pyramids and spheres acted as a wonderful foil for the new breeds of irridescent blue delphiniums, colourful asters and bright dahlias. The informally planted perennials and annuals swaying and dancing in the gentlest of breezes around the static topiary set up a dynamic tension,

Above: The peacock garden at Great Dixter becomes a magical place when hoar-frost thickly covers the yew and densely planted *Aster latiflorus* 'Horizontalis'. The stylized birds that perch on either side of the paved pathway add a simple sophistication to the area while giving it an endearing personality.

adding elegance and depth to the whole.

Topiary has a very important part to play in the contemporary garden, where balance and year-round interest are greatly appreciated. A simple topiary plant can be used to define and give a feeling of stability and permanence. This is because a plant that is clipped into a tight design appears as a living, though immovable, element, always reassuringly the same. Furthermore, topiary can provide sturdy punctuation marks that engender a sense of rhythm. The simplest of shapes can be used to draw the eye to one area of the garden, and a number of uniformly clipped shapes will lead the eye from one area to another.

Topiary can also lighten the mood of a garden considerably. Who could fail to smile at the sight of giant green elephants walking over an immaculate lawn or a teapot appearing over the top of a wall? The way topiary is used is only limited by the gardener's imagination. In Tulcan, Ecuador, there is a cemetery that is entirely composed of walls, arches and obelisks fashioned out of evergreens. The obvious care, dedication and great pride that goes into maintaining the cemetery in this style lends a dignity to it and conveys a sense of reverence for the dead.

Technically it is possible to make a topiary object of any height and width, but the majority of gardeners want something that can be pruned and shaped without the need for an array of ladders and scaffolding. Usually it is best to purchase a plant that is as near as possible to the desired height of the piece to be sculpted. Yew is ideal to use in cool climates, and cypress in warmer ones, as both grow slowly enough not to require too frequent trimmings, and each grows happily into a dense mass.

It is wise to start with simple shapes, such as a pyramid, cone, spiral, sphere or standard, as these are relatively easy to maintain and look remarkably good set amongst a wide array of plants. Their solid block of colour will emphasize the various

leaf shapes of the surrounding perennials and annuals, while at the same time complementing the different flower colours. In autumn and winter, a well-styled object can hold an untidy garden together.

Large shapes are often grown over a metal or wooden frame, giving the novice, and the topiary expert, a constant guide. Ready-made frames can be purchased, or they can easily be made at home out of canes, willow withies or galvanized garden wire. Sometimes a shapeless yew, box or cypress is simply asking to become a handsome peacock. If the plant is pretty well grown, the gardener has to be quite ruthless. A large peacock can only be created by cutting out the central leader, or stem, in order to get the correct shape. It is also important to remember that a plant's natural inclination is to seek the light; for this reason, any shaped plant should always be wider at the base than at the top. If it is not, the growth that is constantly shaded will eventually die back and turn brown. Topiary in pots can be turned periodically to ensure even growth.

Left: The height provided by these two standard box bushes transforms the parterre in which they are planted into a three-dimensional design. Their inclusion helps the parterre to relate more closely to the nearby ancient walls, and lends it a dignified, traditional character.

Opposite: In the dryness of the Mediterranean, this textural planting appears refreshingly green. Massed, clipped mounds of *Santolina rosmarinifolia* surround a classically shaped urn. *Santolina chamaecyparissus*, with its small grey leaves, makes an ideal edging plant with which to frame the design. In mid-summer both santolinas will produce a mass of yellow flowers transforming the garden for a few short weeks into a sea of dancing gold.

GREEN ROOMS

In Europe, during the 19th century, it was very fashionable to design arbours, rooms and tunnels using evergreen shrubs, limes or hornbeam. In a garden that is entirely overlooked by its neighbours, creating a living wall around the garden dramatically alters the character of the plot. The young trees should be planted within a framework; it can be one designed to be seen or one that is positioned so that as the plants became sturdy and take on the style required, it becomes lost from view amongst the foliage. To help make the whole structure solid, horizontal branches on adjoining plants should be pleached or tied together. A construction of this sort can be entirely free-standing, and in time it will become quite rigid.

Right: A solid beech hedge that protects a hillside garden from wild winds has been given a tall narrow 'window' so that the views beyond the enclosed plot can be enjoyed. Placing an urn immediately on the other side of the hedge dresses the archway and reinforces its purpose.

Centre: This aerial view clearly shows the wonderfully shaped walls of this pool room, which curve slightly outwards and upwards away from the central pool, much as the petals of a flower would open.

Cypress or yew can also be used to construct a tree house in the fullest sense of the word, by planting individual trees in a large circle and, as they grow, unobtrusively weaving the branches of one tree together with those of its neighbours (known as plashing) to form a solid structure. Pleaching is decorative shaping and meant to be viewed – it is obviously shaped. Windows and doors can then be cut in these verdant partitions and, as the structure grows in height, different wooden levels, accessed by ladders, can be constructed within them.

Without going to the length of constructing such a tree house, one can enrich an evergreen hedge simply by cutting a window in it at a strategic place so that it frames a view beyond the garden.

Right: A beautifully sculpted box and stone seat set amongst roughly trimmed box hedges invites the visitor to relax and enjoy the tranquillity of the garden. The evergreen climber behind the seat has been trained and cut so that it covers the wall smoothly and densely to make the perfect backdrop.

Left: A series of cypresses grown into tall, gently curved arches stamps this pathway with a unique character that is both superior and inviting. The trees' importance implies that the visitors' destination is one of great interest.

Another way of enlivening a straight hedge is to shape its top into long, sweeping curves. This is especially appealing when the hedge encloses a rigidly geometric plot. It brings a gentleness and movement to the area while at the same time slowing down the wind more effectively than a plain straight hedge would.

Seats can be made out of clipped evergreen shrubs. They are usually bulkier than a normal seat but add a delightful medieval touch to a garden. The actual seat can be made either of turf or of wooden planks, while the back of the seat provides an opportunity to show off the gardener's plant-sculpting skills: it can be low and slightly curved or high and quite elaborate, with swirls or cut-outs.

PARTERRES

Parterres are essentially geometric in character and should be designed on graph paper or with the aid of a computer. They are made by planting dwarf box or a similar low, slow-growing shrub every 20-25cm (8-10in) to form a particular pattern, after preparing the soil well and digging in plenty of humus. Box parterres only require clipping once or twice a year, and this should never be done after early autumn. Clipping encourages new growth and any new growth put on in late autumn will be sappy and liable to frost damage. Herbs look particularly attractive when enclosed by low box hedges. Planting a different herb in each section makes a clear pattern and imparts a feeling of generosity to the whole.

Above: A small formal island bed, surrounded by low growing clipped box, makes an eye-catching feature of deep coloured tulips in spring.

Right: A very ordinary courtyard has been transformed into an interesting and sophisticated space by creating a simple parterre. The energy of the space can be altered by changing the plants that fill the beds. The primulas give the area a feeling of calm, but this would change to one of liveliness if they were replaced with red Busy lizzie (*Impatiens walleriana*).

Low evergreen hedges or parterres are a very useful design tool. They bring a touch of elegance, form and style that can only be beneficial to a garden. A parterre is a geometrically composed design of low hedges, with the spaces between them filled with flowers, originally designed to be seen from the upper windows of a large house. During the 17th century many different styles evolved. In some, the hedges surrounded coloured earth; this type of parterre is particularly suited today to arid situations such as inner city courtyards, where office workers can look down on a pleasing pattern, and to hot, dry climates where water resources are usually restricted.

The most commonly seen parterre though is that contrived from low box hedges that surround flowering plants. This design is informal and most easily transposed to small gardens. Indeed, a parterre blends beautifully with the architecture of country buildings and with inner city 19th-century houses that are tall, sophisticated and elegant but which have small enclosed gardens. A well-executed parterre, composed of neat box hedges in simple, clear shapes which are filled with a single planting of cyclamen or impatiens, enhances a plot. The paths between the hedges can be covered with a good coloured gravel chipping which would harmonize with the colour of the nearby building or with the most dominant plant colour. This has the advantage of providing additional colour in winter, and is easy to walk on in all weathers, unlike grass paths.

A knot garden was traditionally one where the low hedges of evergreen plants were designed in bands which crossed over each other in the same way as a cord or rope makes a knot. To show up the different interweaving bands, different coloured evergreen shrubs were used – dark green box being interwoven with a lighter variegated type. The gaps in the design were filled with herbs or flowers in a similar way to a parterre. As this type of design is quite complicated, many gardeners prefer to restrict themselves to making a simple parterre.

Left: This highly stylized garden room is full of interest and vitality. The low geometrically designed maze has been embellished with lighter square box cones. Placing large box balls on either side of an arbour has counterbalanced the rigidity of these elements, while ivy, trained over a decorative iron frame, embellishes the seating area.

CLOUD PRUNING

This is a type of pruning which in some ways is similar to topiary, but which has a special place in Japanese gardens. In medieval times the Japanese greatly admired all things Chinese, and many Japanese artists travelled to China to learn the precise art of scroll painting. Scrolls depicted stylized trees that had been shaped by the wind. The Japanese then transposed these trees to their gardens, and clipped them to mirror those on the scroll paintings. This became known as cloud pruning.

Above: Three Japanese cloud-pruned trees together form a partial screen. Carefully pruned to keep the same size and shape from one year to another, they give no hint of their age. Their unchanging appearance imparts the feeling of timelessness that is the hallmark of a Japanese garden, while their definite personality gives the area a strength and solidity that is infinitely reassuring.

The Japanese design their gardens on the principle of harmony with nature, and prefer them to be asymmetrical, as they think this emulates nature better than a more symmetrical design would. For this reason a tree trunk should not be completely straight, but rather bent at an angle, as though shaped thus by the wind.

Branches too are shaped at irregular angles, by tying bamboo canes to them for up to three years, or until the branch is set into the required shape. Strings are attached to new delicate branches to encourage them to grow in the right direction. Leaves are pruned away to leave gently rounded balls of growth. These are clipped into different sizes and are designed to appear like the spherical clouds seen on a summer's day, hence the term 'cloud pruning'.

Ilex crenata is ideally suited to this type of treatment, as it is evergreen, slow-growing and has tiny leaves, which helps the 'clouds' to appear smooth and compact. Pine trees are also good subjects. When they are cloud pruned their flower spikes are removed, so that their inherently simple shape is not confused by a later proliferation of cones. Their needles are then trimmed to emphasize the roundness of each 'cloud' and give it a denser appearance.

Hedges can be cloud pruned, and in Japan azalea hedges are often given this treatment, which makes them appear like billowing clouds on the horizon. When they flower they then look like the sky at sunset, and their rolling shape brings a sense of movement to a garden at all times. A box hedge also has a tendency to grow into this style when it has been clipped repeatedly over a great many years.

Because cloud pruning gives a shrub an abstract shape, it is ideal for contemporary Western gardens. Cloud-pruned shrubs have a freshness that is well suited to the clear straight lines of contemporary buildings and their asymmetrical shape adds a feeling of harmony and tranquillity.

Left: A meticulously trained and cloud-pruned tree stands out against the simple plain wall behind it. It is similar in style to those on willow-pattern plates and is a mirror copy of highly popular Chinese scroll-painting trees that have bent trunks and an uneven number of branches.

Above: Japanese trees are thought to be more decorative and beautiful when their branches are set at an angle. Bamboo canes are tied to the branches with soft black twine to train them into the ideal shape – one which replicates a wind-blown tree.

FEATHER PRUNING

Japanese gardens mostly rely on the shape and texture of non-flowering plants for interest, and because of this they have many well-shaped shrubs, which give them an atmosphere that is settled, tranquil and well structured. Besides cloud pruning, the Japanese 'feather prune' some trees and shrubs, and in particular their great favourite, *Acer palmatum*. This small tree varies a great deal in leaf colour and shape, but its five- or seven-lobed leaves are often very delicate, especially *Acer palmatum* 'Crimson Queen' and *A. p.* 'Dissectum'. Feather pruning is used to enhance and emphasize the lacy nature of the leaves and it turns the plant into a delightful, ethereal object, whereas it would otherwise appear as a quite dense-growing tree or shrub.

Below: Here a feather-pruned *Acer palmatum* displays its dark, bent, twisted branches through a lacy curtain of leaves. With superfluous branches and leaves removed, the true nature of the shrub is revealed; when its leaves are wet with morning dew, it becomes an object of infinite beauty.

The first task when shaping an acer is to decide which main branches (three or five) that emerge from the main trunk should be retained. These should appear to be positioned asymmetrically, that is, not evenly spaced. All other branches should be pruned right back to the main stem. Next, all the twiggy branches that cross each other should be removed from the remaining main branches. This reduces the growth considerably, so that only a three- or five-branched skeleton is left, seemingly supporting a clear tracery of small twigs. During the growing season leaves are pinched out so that only a lacework of leaves covers the plant. This results in drawing attention to the real character of the leaves.

When covered in rain or morning dew, a feather-pruned tree or shrub becomes a magically sculptural object. Each leaf tip holds a bead of moisture that glistens and catches the light, making the plant look as though it is covered in gossamer jewel-encrusted material, and even in the depths of winter it retains an appealingly delicate appearance.

Feather pruning has a beneficial effect on the ground beneath the shrub. Because the tree's canopy is not as dense as it would usually be, more sunlight can filter through, making it possible to grow a wider range of plants at the base of the tree. Light shade-loving erythronium, trillium, hosta and viola all would grow happily in the gentle light found under a feather-pruned tree or shrub.

OTHER KINDS OF PRUNING

Even without cloud or feather pruning, it is possible to give most trees and shrubs a more defined shape by paying them just a little care and attention.

A plant that has an attractively shaped trunk and crown subtly gives a garden a feeling of purpose. Trees with clear single trunks, devoid of twiggy projections, whether they are curved or straight, look more sculptural. The area around their base is ideal for growing shade-loving plants whose leaves can enhance the texture of the trunk. Many shrubs, such as various forms of buddleja, naturally throw up many low-growing branches that give them an ill-defined shape; such plants look far more attractive after judicious pruning. All lower branches should be cut hard back to the main stem and any tiny shoots appearing along the trunk and branches that remain should be brushed off by running a gloved hand downwards over the bark. The gardener should aim to produce a plant with a well-proportioned trunk and an attractively styled crown. Drastic pruning is best carried out in the winter when the gardener is able to see more clearly which branches cross each other and should be removed. As the sap is not rising, disease is less likely to enter through any cuts. Ruthlessly pruning a shrub in order to achieve a pleasing overall shape can mean that the shrub or tree might not flower the first spring or summer after, but it is well worth losing one year's blossom to gain a beautifully styled plant.

Above: Here, a simple pathway has been elevated into a special area by planting a series of limes with elegant straight trunks closely together. Their crowns have been trimmed into wedge shapes, which gives them a style and dignity that is reminiscent of medieval cloistered gardens.

Above: The corner of this courtyard has been given an elegant touch by training a hawthorn (*Crataegus laevigata*) into a tall standard. The planting at its feet of a dark pink weigela balances its crown, while its height gives the area a sense of perspective and scale.

Opposite: Subtlety is the hallmark of this enclosed area. The eye is drawn to the statue and then passes onto the delightfully trained corkscrew trunk of the standard bay tree. Shaped yew and box, together with trailing variegated ivy, are in keeping with the brick and moss ground-cover.

STANDARDS

Many plants lend themselves to being shaped into a standard. A standard is a shrub which has a single central stem topped by a loose growth of stems, unlike topiary, where the head is solid. With patience any gardener can train a plant into a handsome standard, though most plants will take several years to do so.

A standard acts as a punctuation mark when placed amongst low-growing plants; it also provides a good vertical point amongst small plants. Patios and paved areas are often devoid of tall plants, and in such areas container-grown standard shrubs have an invaluable part to play. A collection of different-sized container-grown standards offers the possibility of changing the perspective from time to time by rearranging them, thus giving the whole area an entirely new look. In the smallest of spaces, they bring an air of elegance and romance. Before deciding on the eventual height of a proposed standard, you will do well to remember that its head should be in proportion to the size of the container. Heavy foliage on top of a long stem will attract wind rock if the container is not large enough. The more foliage the plant can boast, the larger the container should be, and in some cases the shorter the stem.

It is possible to purchase many types of ready-made standard shrubs; roses, wisteria and *Brugmansia aurea* are particularly attractive when trained in this fashion. A large container-grown *Brugmansia aurea* will add an exotic touch to the simplest of gardens, with its large, well-shaped trumpet flowers. Placed at either end of a bench they will entice the visitor to sit down. A wisteria

Above: A series of standard-trained wisterias add elegance to this private garden. When you grow it in this manner, you get the full benefit of the delicate fragrance of the drooping racemes of flowers. Here the profusion of flowers demonstrates that wisteria is just as happy to be grown in this way as it is to be trained over the front of a house.

also looks particularly fine treated in this way, rather than trained up over an arch or along the side of a house, as it gives one the added advantage of being able to smell its wonderfully fragrant flowers. Wisteria develops faster when it is grafted onto a cultivar such as *Wisteria floribunda*, which might be more expensive but is well worth the extra cost. Having bought a healthy plant on a good cultivar, the main stem or leader has to be cut back by one third, and all side shoots must be removed before tying it to a good straight cane or stake. Over the next few years the plant has to be summer- and winter-pruned to restrict its growth in order to build up a healthy and sturdy framework. Many other flowering plants can be treated in a similar manner.

Standard lemon and orange trees add height and elegance to a parterre that might otherwise appear uniform and a bit dull.

Other fruit trees also look highly decorative grown as standards. A fig tree is ideal as it loves to have its roots restricted by a container. A newly purchased fruit plant should be tied to a straight cane and all side shoots removed. Once it has grown to the desired height the main tip should be pinched out to encourage side shoots to grow. These have their growth restricted by tip pruning once they have grown five or six leaves. Any additional growth along the stem should be rubbed off so that it appears clean. After roughly three years the gardener will have a decorative standard that should provide good fruit.

CORDONS AND ESPALIERS

In a small garden, fruit trees can be grown and trained in a great variety of styles to provide architectural features. An espalier is a tree that is single-stemmed with evenly spaced lateral branches that have been trained along wires. These are pruned so that the new growth is severely restricted, making the whole plant compact. Where a garden needs to be divided in a light-handed way, fruit trees trained in this fashion provide a living and open wall that will have the added advantage of producing an abundance of fruit.

A cordon, which is a single-stemmed fruit tree that has all its lateral shoots severely pruned so that they appear as clusters of growth along the stem, is ideal for growing round arches. Indeed, a series of cordons can be grown over arches to form a fruit tunnel. This can be a real architectural, design feature in a garden and the placing of it should be carefully considered. Such a tunnel would look attractive at the top of a flight of steps, where it would serve to link one area of the garden with another. Cordon arches might be placed around a lawn to give it an enclosed feeling, whilst allowing a glimpse of it. Alternatively, a single cordon arch set at the entrance of a vegetable garden would add an air of sophistication, and counter-balance the straight rows of vegetables.

Where a flower border or vegetable bed needs to be edged, a series of fairly low, step-over cordons is ideal. Each cordon is made up of a single-tiered espalier fruit tree trained to be no more than 46-60cm (18in-2ft) high, with a short central stem and two lateral branches trained in a straight line. The cordons will help to create a sense of harmony while providing an interesting and decorative edging.

Above: A Gloucestershire *potager* is made more decorative by training an apple tree as an espalier against the warm, mellow stone wall. The added advantage of this stylish method of growing fruit is that even in a small space you can get the benefit of a full crop of fruit.

Left: A flowering apple-tree tunnel is a truly magical place. To be surrounded by the delicate white, rose-flushed flowers, alive with honey bees, is an intensely pleasurable experience. This wide tunnel has been created by training single cordons up and around the thin supporting ironwork structure. In time, the apple trees will become rigid enough on their own to withstand the strongest winds and still produce an abundance of fruit.

Above: Cordon apple trees form an integral part of the design of this herb garden. Geometrically shaped dense box hedging is complemented by the more open character of the apple trees; together they impart a textural feel to the plot. Cordons of this height make the harvesting of fruit a much simpler matter than with normal height trees.

5
Sculpture
in the
Garden

A WELL-TENDED, MUCH-LOVED GARDEN has a warm, inviting atmosphere. One way of signalling its value is to place one or two carefully selected sculptures among a group of favourite plants. An object chosen with passion and placed with care will infuse the area surrounding it with an intangible aura that survives for as long as that object remains in place. When archaeologists discover the remains of a stone figurine in an ancient garden, they understand the importance it held for someone. Immediately the site becomes personal to the man or woman who chose to place that piece in that particular spot.

Sculpture helps to create a style and can be used to strengthen a garden design. All of us unconsciously associate a certain type of sculpture with a particular kind of garden. Neatly trimmed yew or box hedges, for example, with a classical stone urn placed on a plinth at the end of a grass path, strongly convey an Italian style; at the same time the urn provides a distinct, strong, focal point. Sculptures are also a useful tool for creating a sense of scale in a garden. Like designer plants, they can add height or width to an area, when placed with careful consideration.

Left: A simple urn placed beyond the end of a pathway acts as an important focal point. It invites the visitors to make their way along the path to take a closer look at it, and elevates the importance of the path.

STONE STATUES AND OBJECTS

An added sense of period and time can be introduced with the use of stone statues. Their elegant form is a pleasing reminder of man's ability to tame nature, thereby heightening the garden's appeal. A rustic stone figure, such as a shepherdess, set among a naturalistic planting of trees and shrubs will call to mind an 18th-century garden, when the vogue was for a manicured landscape of contrived rural simplicity.

Above: A tiny clearing surrounded by old-fashioned roses, heavy with scent, has been transformed into a special and secret space by positioning a handsome dry-stone urn sculpture in a central position within it. The classical shape and the bluish-grey colour of the stone complements the lax and gentle nature of the roses.

Left: Placing a decorative marble Grecian bust in amongst the flowers in this mixed border has given it a highly individual personality. The sophisticated character of the sculpture acts as a link between the formal box cones and the randomly planted perennials and tulips, thereby pulling the different elements together to make a cohesive whole.

Over-sized sculptural pieces are often employed to make the onlooker feel small and vulnerable. Stately gardens used this ploy in the past to infuse an estate with a feeling of importance and grandeur, which in turn made the common man feel somewhat insignificant. Small objects, on the other hand, are useful for producing the opposite effect, making a plot feel human, friendly and comfortable. A small stone ball or stone lion placed amongst just one or two plants

Above: In the verdant depths of this garden, two classically designed stone columns support a number of climbing vines. Their size and dignified style imparts a captivating feeling of faded grandeur to the area. The columns suggest that time has passed this quiet spot by, and that the plants have progressively engulfed them.

will enhance their shape and impart a sense of unity to them.

There are endless sculptural and architectural objects to choose from. Before making any purchase, try to analyze what elements the garden lacks that might be improved by such an object. Does the plot lack a good focal point? Is there no visual interest in winter? Perhaps the garden blends so well with the surrounding landscape that it needs a humanizing touch to strengthen its

link to the house? Placing the right architectural object in the correct place can solve all these problems.

Classical shapes convey tranquillity and permanence. A single quality piece will impart an air of elegance to even the simplest and smallest of gardens. A beautiful Grecian-style urn placed between clipped dark yew hedges elevates them, making them appear strong. Weather-worn remains of classical columns half-hidden in long grass will invoke a feeling of history, implying the remains of a long-lost civilization, while the untended character of the rest of the area helps to emphasize the sophistication of the artefacts. Discovering such objects strewn amongst wild flowers and surrounded by trees can startle the visitor into seeing the shapes of the surrounding vegetation with fresh eyes.

A hot, dry Mediterranean garden calls out for the soothing qualities of running water. A large Cretan pot, adapted as a fountain on a bed of pebbles or in a shallow pool, will provide this, while reinforcing the classical simplicity of nearby buildings. The pot should be fitted with a pump to circulate water so that it continuously flows over its rim and back down to the ground.

Above: Decorative features are an intricate part of a Japanese garden, which relies heavily on foliage plants for additional year-round interest. A traditionally shaped circular stone water bowl and bamboo water spout set amongst humble ferns signal to the visitor that they have entered a special area of the garden.

SCULPTING WITH NATURAL RESOURCES

Opposite: Two swans, made out of willow and bamboo leaves, give a pond life and vitality in a naturalistic style. Constructed from organic material rather than from metal, they have a gentleness that is attractive and well suited to their surroundings. They have a strong visual appeal that transforms the pond into a place of magic and beauty.

As gardens have become increasingly important to people of all ages, and are often considered to be an extension of their home, many people, with growing confidence, have started creating their own sculpture within them. With the awareness of conservation and a greater respect for the environment, attention has become increasingly focused on the use of natural materials. A great many sculptors and craftspeople have turned to fashioning unique objects from natural materials such as willow or hazel. Although these natural objects are not as enduring as stone, they are certainly more relaxed, suiting the setting of a more casual garden.

Above: Sculpted willow geese humanize this area of garden and give it a strongly individual personality that is both humorous and interesting. The realistic shapes and natural material used to construct the geese infuses the simply planted space with a feeling of gentle harmony that is captivating.

Willow withies can be woven into any shape, as they are light, flexible and easy to handle. There are different types of willow that vary in colour from a rich brown-red to apple green; these different shades can be used to form different parts of an object. Willow can be woven into animals, large life-like figures, and sculptural, abstract shapes. Their lightness makes them perfect for the casual garden where only a suggestion of human activity is needed. In a wild garden, a willow deer or goose reinforces the rural theme while introducing a feeling of proportion to the area. The size of the willow animal acts as a visual aid to measuring the depth and breadth of the surrounding space. A large animal placed in a small clearing will call attention to the restrictions of space, while a small object will provide the illusion of a larger plot.

Willow can also be made into obelisks and wigwams, ideal for a cottage garden or a vegetable plot. They instantly provide tall focal points, while their open framework retains the feeling of airiness. They are suited to supporting climbers such as sweet peas (*Lathyrus*), the morning glory vine (*Ipomoea*), and twining snapdragon (*Asarina*).

WOODEN ARCHITECTURAL FEATURES

Wooden objects have an understated simplicity that is particularly suited to quiet, natural gardens. The beauty of wood becomes more obvious with age; as it weathers, it acquires a mellowness that reveals the grain. It is important to remember that wooden sculptural objects should be elevated slightly so that their base does not rot. A carved animal or figure in wood has a warm quality whatever its size. A town garden could have its jungle theme reinforced by placing a large wooden panther amongst lush leaves, the relationship between the size of the leaves and that of the creature giving a feeling of scale to the overall plot.

Unpainted wooden obelisks, even if they are large, tend to merge into their surroundings. They are easy on the eye, making it possible for the gaze to flick past them to objects that are showier. However, such wooden obelisks are also well-suited to painting, and they give the gardener an opportunity of introducing architectural features together with colour. In confined gardens especially, winter can be a visually bleak time of year and this can be partially rectified by painting obelisks of varying heights. A short garden could be made to appear longer by placing a tall obelisk close to the house, a medium-sized one halfway down the garden, and, finally, a small one furthest from the house. Providing the planting is also arranged in this way, the garden will appear more extensive than is actually the case. If the obelisks are painted the same colour they also become unifying focal points.

If you paint an architectural feature, choose an appropriate colour for the object to enhance its style. It should not jar the eye or dominate an area, but should sit comfortably in its setting and unify the design of the garden. Hot dry gardens which largely rely on succulents, cacti or grey-leaved plants can be given greater focus by adding a painted wooden sculptural object to the area. In a contemporary garden, vivid brightly coloured wooden plant supports or trellis help to create a balance with any strong architectural features, such as nearby buildings, forming a dynamic whole. Pale green adds natural colour to a garden in winter when there is less greenery and more shades of brown. In summer it blends into the surrounding symphony of plants and in no way at all detracts from their leaf shapes or beautiful flowers.

Right: Placing a gigantic wooden sculpted toadstool on top of a tree stump has eased the stark brutality of a felled mature tree. Acquiring this handsome carving lessens the sadness associated with losing a beautiful, old and loved tree and has partially filled the visual gap made by its removal.

METAL SCULPTURES

Almost any metal object can be used as sculpture in the garden, providing it is placed in the correct situation. Metal objects can be representative of an industrial age and of man's efforts to conquer nature. Rusting machinery left lying amongst wild flowers is a reminder that plants renew themselves in the most wonderful way and this energy is magnified by the solidity of the discarded machinery.

Mystery can be planted as surely as any plant, and can be achieved by using man-made objects. Japanese gardens frequently have one or two graceful cranes at the edge of a limpid pond. Acting as focal points, they remind the viewer of the myth that cranes once carried people to an island of immortality.

Blacksmiths are skilled in making large sculptural pieces that add dynamic energy; encouraged by the growing demand for their work, many are exploring new techniques to produce innovative architectural items. Polished bronze and sheet metal reflect the light and pulsate with a life of their own. Beautifully forged iron gazebos, obelisks and arches add elegance and sophistication to a garden. Their inherent solidity makes them eminently suitable as permanent structures, but at the same time their delicate open style makes them useful focal points in a small garden, as they are not over-dominant. A gazebo inevitably adds a romantic touch, especially when smothered with scented roses and pretty clematis, demonstrating clearly the positive visual and emotional benefits of using architectural elements within a garden.

Above: A simple iron sundial positioned amongst deep purple lavender adds height and a sense of scale to the planting. It draws the eye to the area where its strong, dark lines stand out against the gentle outlines of the *Lavandula angustifolia* 'Imperial Gem' that surrounds it and of the apple-green lovage behind.

6 Plant Directory

THE FOLLOWING PLANT DIRECTORY is a guide to those plants, including trees and shrubs, that are most useful in architectural terms, being highly distinctive. It is not a definitive list, but the plants included should be commonly available from good nurseries.

Plants are listed alphabetically by Latin name, with the common name in brackets. Each plant is categorized by type, by the minimum temperature it will tolerate, by soil preference and by light needs. The height and spread of each plant is given in both metric and imperial measurements; it indicates the eventual size the plant may reach in anything from two to 20 years. Grown in ideal conditions, a plant may reach its full height and width in half the time that it would take in a poorer situation.

The hardiness rating is a rough guide only. All gardens have hot and cold spots, making it possible to grow a plant in one position but not in another. Other factors that affect hardiness are wind chill and moisture. The golden rule is to seek out specialist nurseries and to follow their cultural advice.

Note: A few plants are poisonous (or have parts that are poisonous) if ingested; others may cause skin rashes. Take care with planting where there are young children and seek advice from a reputable nursery.

Left: The evening sunlight, catching the seed-heads of Cardoon (*Cynara cardunculus*), *Cortaderia selloana* 'Pumila' and *Kniphofia rooperi*, highlights the architectural qualities of each plant, turning the whole into a spectacular yet mellow display.

Acanthus mollis
(Bear's breeches)
Semi-evergreen herbaceous
upright perennial. Dark glossy
green leaves and spires of
hooded mauve-pink flowers in
late summer.
FULLY HARDY; **SOIL:** WELL-DRAINED;
POSITION: FULL SUN TO LIGHT SHADE
H x S 1.2m x 90cm (4ft x 30in)

ACER
A. griseum (Paperbark maple)
Spreading tree grown for its
orange-brown bark. Green
palmate leaves give good
autumn colour.
FULLY HARDY; **SOIL:** MOIST, FERTILE;
POSITION: FULL SUN TO LIGHT SHADE
H 10m (32ft)

**A. palmatum 'Crimson
Queen'** (Japanese maple)
Deciduous shrub or tree.
Grown for its leaves, which may
vary in colour but are mainly
red-purple in appearance. The
autumn produces brilliant colour.
FULLY HARDY; **SOIL:** ACID;
POSITION: SUN
H x S 3 x 4m (10 x 13ft)

**A.p. 'Dissectum
Atropurpureum'**
Deciduous, mound-forming
shrub. Lacy, deeply divided
leaves, which produce red-
purple colours. The autumn
produces brilliant colour.
FULLY HARDY; **SOIL:** ACID, MOIST BUT
WELL-DRAINED; **POSITION:** SUN
H x S 1.5 x 1.5m (5 x 5ft)

**Aeonium arboreum 'Arnold
Schwarzkopf'**
Bushy succulent perennial.
Mainly grown for its stunning
rosettes of purple-black leaves.
Golden pyramids of flowers in
late spring.
TENDER; **SOIL:** FERTILE, WELL-DRAINED;
POSITION: SUN TO LIGHT SHADE
H x S 60cm x 2m (2 x 6ft)

Agapanthus
Genus of clump-forming
perennials, some evergreen.
Strap-shaped leaves. Large
umbels of bell-shaped
flowers, blue, white and
purple borne on single
stems in summer.
HARDY TO FROST HARDY; **SOIL:** MOIST,
WELL-DRAINED; **POSITION:** FULL SUN
H x S 1m x 50cm (3ft x 20in)

Agave americana
(Century plant)
Perennial succulent. Very long,
fleshy, sword-shaped leaves.
Dense spikes of bell-shaped
white to pale, creamy yellow
flowers in spring to summer.
HALF-HARDY; **SOIL:** SLIGHTLY ACID,
WELL-DRAINED; **POSITION:** SUN
H x S 1-1.8 x 1.8-3m (3-6 x 6-10ft)

Ailanthus altissima
(Tree of heaven)
Fast-growing, deciduous,
spreading tree. Lance-shaped
leaflets in reddish-brown, turning
to dark green. Large clusters of
small green flowers in summer,
followed by reddish-brown
winged fruits in autumn. Its
pollen can cause an allergic
reaction. Tolerates pollution well.
FULLY HARDY; **SOIL:** DEEP, FERTILE,
WELL-DRAINED; **POSITION:** SUN TO
LIGHT SHADE
H x S 25 x 15m (80 x 50ft)

Akebia quinata
(Chocolate vine)
Woody-stemmed, twining, semi-
evergreen climber. Mid-green
leaves are composed of palmate
leaflets. Maroon chocolate-
scented flowers in late spring
followed by purplish fruits.
FROST HARDY; **SOIL:** MOIST, WELL-
DRAINED; **POSITION:** SUN TO LIGHT
PARTIAL SHADE
H 10m (32ft)

ANGELICA
A. archangelica officinalis
(Angelica)
Upright perennial, often grown
as a biennial. Large, deeply
divided mid-green leaves.
Umbels of white or green flowers
in late summer.
FULLY HARDY; **SOIL:** DEEP, MOIST;
POSITION: SUN TO PARTIAL SHADE
H x S 1.8 x 1.2m (6 x 4ft)

A. gigas
Short-lived perennial, often
grown as a biennial. Large,
lobed, mid-green leaves.
Maroon flowers in early to
mid-summer.
FULLY HARDY; **SOIL:** DEEP, MOIST, WELL-
DRAINED; **POSITION:** SUN OR SHADE
H x S 1-1.8 x 1.2m (3-6 x 4ft)

Arbutus menziesii (Madrona)
Evergreen spreading tree.
Vibrant red peeling bark and

Above: *Sedum dendroideum* and *Agave americana*

glossy, dark green, oval leaves.
Upright panicles of urn-shaped
white flowers in early summer,
followed by orange or red fruit.
FROST HARDY; **SOIL:** ACID, WELL-
DRAINED; **POSITION:** SUN
H 18m (60 ft)

**Archontophoenix
cunninghamiana**
(Illawarra palm, Piccabeen palm)
Evergreen palm tree. Mid-green,
pinnate, frond-like leaves.
Clusters of small lavender or lilac
flowers in summer.
TENDER; **SOIL:** FERTILE, MOIST, WELL-
DRAINED; **POSITION:** SUN TO PARTIAL
SHADE
H x S 15-20 x 1.8-5m
(50-70 x 6-15ft)

Armeria maritima (Sea thrift)
Evergreen, clump-forming
perennial. Dark green, grass-like
narrow leaves. Stiff stems carry
round heads of small, white to

pink flowers in summer.
FULLY HARDY; **SOIL:** WELL-DRAINED;
POSITION: SUN
H x S 10 x 15cm (4 x 6in)

Arum italicum
(Large cuckoo-pint)
Tuberous perennial. Spear-
shaped dark green leaves with
silver marbling. Pale green or
creamy white spathes of flowers
in late spring, red berries in
autumn.
FROST HARDY; **SOIL:** RICH, WELL-
DRAINED; **POSITION:** SUN TO PARTIAL
SHADE
H x S 15 x 25cm (6 x 12in)

Atriplex hortensis var. **rubra**
(Red mountain spinach)
Erect, fast-growing annual.
Spear-shaped maroon, edible
leaves.
HALF-HARDY; **SOIL:** MOIST, WELL-
DRAINED; **POSITION:** SUN
H x S 2m x 30cm (6 x 1ft)

Bergenia (Elephant's ears)
Evergreen perennial. Thick rounded to oval leaves.
FULLY HARDY; SOIL: RICH, MOIST; POSITION: SUN, PARTIAL SHADE
H x S up to 45 x 60cm (18in x 2ft)

BETULA (Birch)
B. ermanii 'Grayswood Hill'
Deciduous tree. Decorative peeling pure white bark. Produces catkins in spring.
FULLY HARDY; SOIL: MOIST, WELL-DRAINED; POSITION: SUN
H 20m (70ft)

B. utilis jacquemontii 'Greyshill Ghost'
(Himalayan birch)
Similar to the above, but slightly smaller.
FULLY HARDY; SOIL: MOIST, WELL-DRAINED; POSITION: SUN, LIGHT SHADE
H 18m (60ft)

Brahea armata (Blue-fan palm)
Evergreen palm. Fan-shaped leaves.
TENDER; SOIL: WELL-DRAINED; POSITION: SUN
H x S 12 x 7m (40 x 21ft)

Brugmansia aurea
Evergreen rounded shrub or tree. Oval leaves and pendant, trumpet-shaped white or yellow flowers 15-25cm (6-10in) long in late summer, early autumn.
FROST TENDER, MIN. TEMP. 7ºC (45ºF); SOIL: FERTILE, WELL-DRAINED; POSITION: SUN
H 5-10m (15-30ft)

Buxus sempervirens
(Common box)
Evergreen shrub. Small, oblong, dark green leaves. Ideal for hedging, screening and topiary. Prone to new fungus diseases in damp regions (grow *Buxus microphylla* in its stead if you are in such an area).
FULLY HARDY; SOIL: WELL-DRAINED; POSITION: SUN TO PARTIAL SHADE
H x S 5 x 5m (15 x 15ft)

Canna
Genus of rhizomatous perennials grown for their ornamental foliage and flowers.
FROST TENDER, MIN. TEMP. 10-15ºC (50-59ºF). SOIL: HUMUS-RICH, MOIST; POSITION: SUN
H x S 2.2m x 50cm (7ft x 20in)

Cardiocrinum giganteum
(Giant lily)
Statuesque bulbous perennial. Scented white flowers in summer.
FULLY TO FROST HARDY; SOIL: MOIST TO WELL-DRAINED; POSITION: SHADE
H x S 1.5-4m x 45cm (5-13ft x 18in)

Carex comans
(New Zealand hair sedge)
Evergreen sedge.
FULLY HARDY; SOIL: MOIST; POSITION: SUN TO PARTIAL SHADE
H x S 30cm x 1m (1 x 3ft)

Centranthus ruber
(Red valerian)
Perennial forming loose clumps of fleshy leaves. Branching heads of small, star-shaped, deep reddish-pink or white flowers are borne above foliage from late spring to autumn.
FULLY HARDY; SOIL: THRIVES IN POOR, EXPOSED CONDITIONS; POSITION: SUN
H x S 60cm-1m x 45-60cm (2-3ft x 18in-2ft)

Cephlocereus senilis
(Old-man cactus)
Slow-growing columnar perennial cactus. Long, white hair-like covering. Flowers in summer, unlikely to flower in cultivation.
TENDER, MIN. TEMP. 5ºC (41ºF); SOIL: WELL-DRAINED, SLIGHTLY ALKALINE; POSITION: SUN
H x S 15m x 40cm (50ft x 16in)

Cereus forbesii
Columnar, perennial cactus with a branching, blue-green stem bearing dark spines on 4-7 prominent ribs. In summer bears 25cm- (10in-) long, cup-shaped white flowers at night, followed by red fruits.
TENDER, MIN. TEMP. 7ºC (45ºF); SOIL: WELL-DRAINED; POSITION: SUN
H x S 4m x 60cm (12 x 2ft)

Chamaedorea
(Bamboo palm)
Genus of evergreen palms. Arching decorative leaves borne on slender stems.
TENDER; SOIL: MOIST, RICH, WELL-DRAINED, NEUTRAL TO ACID; POSITION: SHADE TO SEMI-SHADE
H x S 1-3m x 50cm-2m (3-10ft x 1.5-6ft)

Choisya ternata
(Mexican orange blossom)
Evergreen rounded shrub. Aromatic, bright green oblong leaves. Clusters of white fragrant flowers in late spring, and often again in late summer to autumn. 'Sundance' has golden foliage.
FROST HARDY; SOIL: FERTILE, WELL-DRAINED; POSITION: SUN
H 2.5m (8ft)

Citrus
Genus of evergreen trees or shrubs. Dark glossy leaves and fragrant flowers from spring to summer.
FROST TENDER; SOIL: MOIST, WELL-DRAINED, NEUTRAL TO ACID; POSITION: SUN TO PARTIAL SHADE
H x S 6-12 x 5m (20-40 x 15ft)

Clematis armandii
Evergreen climber. Long, oblong dark green leaves. Scented, single white flowers in early spring.
FROST HARDY; SOIL: WELL-DRAINED, MOIST; POSITION: FEET IN SHADE, HEAD IN SUN, SHELTER FROM WINDS
H 5m (15ft)

Clivia miniata
Tuft-forming, evergreen, rhizomatous perennial. Strap-shaped, semi-erect, dark green leaves. Stems produce a head of 10-20 orange or red funnel-shaped flowers in late spring, early summer.
FROST TENDER, MIN. TEMP.10ºC (50ºF); SOIL: WELL-DRAINED; POSITION: PARTIAL SHADE
H x S 40 x 30-60cm (16in x 1-2ft)

Colchicum speciosum 'Album'
Perennial corm. Lance-shaped, large, semi-erect leaves in late winter to spring. White, weather-resistant flowers appear separately in autumn.
HALF-HARDY TO FULLY HARDY; SOIL: DEEP, FERTILE, WELL-DRAINED; POSITION: FULL SUN
H x S 18 x 10cm (7 x 4in)

Cordyline fruticosa
(Good luck plant, Ti tree)
Slow-growing, upright, suckering evergreen shrub. Broad, strap-shaped deep green leaves. Branched panicles of small

Below: A blue agapanthus and shaped yew in the background

white, purplish or reddish flowers in summer.
FROST TENDER; **SOIL:** FERTILE, WELL-DRAINED; **POSITION:** SUN TO PARTIAL SHADE
H x S 1.8-4 x 1-1.8m (6-13 x 3-6ft)

Cornus controversa
(Wedding cake tree)
Deciduous layered tree. The tiered branches give it a distinctive shape. Bright green oval leaves turn purple in autumn. Clusters of small, star-shaped, white flowers in early summer.
FULLY HARDY; **SOIL:** RICH, WELL-DRAINED, NEUTRAL TO ACID; **POSITION:** SUN TO PARTIAL SHADE
H 15m (50ft)

Cortaderia selloana
(Pampas grass)
Evergreen clump-forming perennial grass. Erect plume-like silvery panicles borne above long, narrow, sharp-edged mid-green leaves. Female flowers have long, silky hairs in late summer.
FROST HARDY; **SOIL:** FERTILE, WELL-DRAINED; **POSITION:** SUN
H x S 2.5 x 1.2m (8 x 4ft)

CRAMBE
C. cordifolia
Perennial. Mounds of large, crinkled and lobed dark green leaves. Clouds of small, fragrant white flowers borne in branching sprays in late spring to summer.
FULLY HARDY; **SOIL:** FERTILE, WELL-DRAINED; **POSITION:** SUN TO LIGHT SHADE
H x S 1.8 x 1.2m (6 x 4ft)

C. maritima (Sea kale)
Mound-forming herbaceous perennial. Wide, crinkled glaucous, silvery-green leaves. Large heads of small, fragrant, white flowers opening into branching sprays in summer.
FULLY HARDY; **SOIL:** MOIST, WELL-DRAINED; **POSITION:** SUN
H x S 75 x 60cm (30in x 2ft)

CRATAEGUS (Hawthorn)
Genus of deciduous trees and shrubs. Small insignificant leaves with five-petalled flowers in spring and ornamental fruits in autumn.
FULLY HARDY; **SOIL:** ANY, EXCEPT VERY

Right: *Crambe maritima*

WET; **POSITION:** SUN TO PARTIAL SHADE
H x S 6-8 x 6m (18-25 x 18ft)

C. laciniata 'Ucria'
Compact tree. Dark green leaves. White flowers in spring. Orange to red berries in autumn.
FULLY HARDY; **SOIL:** ANY, EXCEPT WATER-LOGGED; **POSITION:** SUN TO PARTIAL SHADE
H x S 6m (20ft)

Cupressus sempervirens
(Italian cypress)
Slender, upright, evergreen tree. Aromatic, grey-green foliage.
HALF-HARDY; **SOIL:** WELL-DRAINED; **POSITION:** SUN
H x S 20 x 1-6m (70 x 3-20ft)

Cycas revoluta
(Japanese sago palm)
Slow-growing evergreen palm-like cycad. May produce several trunks. Has arching fronds, and bears tight clusters of reddish fruits in autumn.
HALF-HARDY; **SOIL:** MOIST, FERTILE, WELL-DRAINED; **POSITION:** SUN
H x S 1-2 x 1-2m (3-6 x 3-6ft)

Cyclamen hederifolium
Perennial tuber. Leaves often ivy-shaped with silvery-green patterns. Pale to deep pink flowers in autumn.
FROST HARDY; **SOIL:** FERTILE, WELL-DRAINED; **POSITION:** SUN TO PARTIAL SHADE
H x S 10 x 15cm (4 x 6in)

CYNARA
C. cardunculus (Cardoon)
Architectural perennial. Clumps of large, pointed, divided silver-grey leaves. Thistle-like blue-purple flowers borne singly on stout grey stems in summer to autumn.
FROST HARDY; **SOIL:** FERTILE, WELL-DRAINED; **POSITION:** SUN AND SHELTER
H x S 1.5 x 1.2m (5 x 4ft)

C. scolymus (Globe artichoke)
Similar to the above, but slightly taller.
FROST HARDY; **SOIL:** FERTILE, WELL-DRAINED; **POSITION:** SUN AND SHELTER
H x S 1.8 x 1.2m (6 x 4ft)

Cyperus involucratus
(Umbrella grass)
Evergreen, tuft-forming perennial. Leaves are green and grass-like. Delicate clustered flowerheads in summer.
HALF-HARDY; **SOIL:** MOIST; **POSITION:** SUN TO PARTIAL SHADE
H x S 1m x 60cm (3 x 2ft)

Cyrtomium falcatum
(Holly fern, Fishtail fern)
Evergreen fern. Fronds are lance-shaped and have holly-like, glossy, dark green pinnae; young fronds are often covered with whitish or brown scales.
HALF HARDY; **SOIL:** MOIST; **POSITION:** PARTIAL SHADE.
H x S 30-60 x 30-45cm (1-2ft x 1ft-18in)

Darmera peltata
(Umbrella plant)
Spreading perennial. Large dark-green rounded leaves, turning red in autumn. Clusters of white or pale pink flowers on white-haired stems in late spring before foliage appears.
FULLY HARDY; **SOIL:** MOIST, BOGGY; **POSITION:** SUN TO PARTIAL SHADE
H x S 1.8 x 1m (6 x 3ft)

Dasylirion longissimum
(Mexican grass plant)
Succulent perennial. Tree-like, angled and fleshy olive green leaves up to 1.5 m (5ft) long. Flowers in summer.
TENDER, MIN. TEMP. 10ºC (50ºF); **SOIL:** WELL-DRAINED; **POSITION:** SUN, SHELTER FROM WINDS
H x S 4 x 1.5m (13 x 5ft)

Dicksonia antarctica
(Australian tree fern)
Semi-evergreen tree-like fern. Stout trunk covered with brown fibres crowned by spreading, much-divided palm-like fronds.
HALF-HARDY; **SOIL:** RICH, ACID, MOIST; **POSITION:** FULL TO PARTIAL SHADE; HUMID ATMOSPHERE
H x S 10 x 4m (32 x 13ft)

Dierama
(Angel's fishing rod; wandflower)
Genus of evergreen, clump-forming corms. Insignificant leaves. Funnel- or bell-shaped flowers on long stems in summer.

Frost tender to half-hardy; **Soil:** Well-drained, moist, flourishes near ponds; **Position:** Sun; shelter from winds
H x S 1-1.8m x 30cm (3-6 x 1ft)

Digitalis purpurea
(Foxglove)
Short-lived perennial, usually grown as a biennial. Tall spikes of tubular flowers in summer.
Fully hardy; **Soil:** Moist, well-drained; **Position:** Semi-shade
H x S 1.5m x 60cm (5ft x 2ft)

Dracaena marginata 'Tricolor'
Slow-growing, evergreen, upright tree or shrub with narrow, strap-shaped, cream-striped, rich green leaves, prominently edged with red.
Tender, Min. temp. 13°C (55°F); **Soil:** Well-drained; **Position:** Sun
H x S 2-5 x 1-3m (6-15 x 3-10ft)

Drimys winteri (Winter's bark)
Upright tree, with aromatic apple-green bark. Lance-shaped tough leaves, green above, off-white beneath. White flower umbels from spring to early summer.
Frost hardy; **Soil:** Fertile, moist, well-drained; **Position:** Shelter from winds
H x S 15 x 10m (50 x 32ft)

Dryopteris
Genus of deciduous or semi-evergreen ferns, with much-divided, mid-green fronds. Many form regular, shuttlecock-like crowns.
Fully to half hardy; **Soil:** Moist; **Position:** Shade
H up to 1m (3ft)

ECHEVERIA
E. agavoides
Evergreen, clump-forming, perennial succulent. Rosettes of stout, fleshy tapering light green leaves. Cup-shaped red flowers in early summer.
Frost tender; **Soil:** Poor, very well-drained; **Position:** Sun
H x S 15 x 30cm (6in x 1ft)

E. lilacina
Evergreen, perennial succulent. Grey fleshy leaves assume their brightest colours from autumn to spring. Long-lasting rosettes of flowers in spring.

Above: *Euphorbia polychroma* and *Epimedium x. rubrum*

Frost tender, Min. temp. 5°C (41°F); **Soil:** Poor, well-drained; **Position:** Sun
H x S 10 x 15cm (4 x 6in)

Echinocactus grusonii
(Golden barrel cactus)
Hemispherical, slow-growing perennial cactus. Woolly crown bears a ring of golden-yellow flowers in summer.
Frost tender, Min. temp. 11°C (52°F); **Soil:** Fertile, well-drained; **Position:** Sun
H x S 1.8 x 1.8m (6 x 6ft)

Echinops (Globe thistle)
Genus of perennials, grown for their blue to white-grey flowers in summer. Greyish-green foliage.
Fully Hardy; **Soil:** Poor, well-drained; **Position:** Full Sun
H x S 1.2-1.8 x1m (4-6 x 3ft)

ECHIUM
E. candicans, E. simplex, E. wildpretii
Evergreen, unbranched, biennial shrubs. Leaves are long, strap-shaped and grey-green. Compact spines of small funnel-shaped flowers from spring to summer.
Half-hardy; **Soil:** Fertile, well-drained; **Position:** Sun
H x S 2.5m x 60cm (8 x 2ft)

Epimedium x rubrum
(Bishop's hat)
Carpeting perennial. Leaves grow densely and are heart-shaped, divided and dark brownish-red in spring. Clusters of small cup-shaped crimson flowers in spring.
Fully Hardy; **Soil:** Moist, fertile, well-drained; **Position:** Partial shade
H x S 20 x 30cm (8in x 1ft)

Eremurus (Foxtail lily)
Perennial. Tall leafless stems of racemes. *E. robustus* has pink flowers, *E. himalaicus* has white.
Fully hardy (when adult); **Soil:** Fertile, well drained; **Position:** Full

Sun and shelter from winds
H x S 1.2-1.8m x 60cm (4-6 x 2ft)

Eryngium (Sea holly)
Genus of rosette-forming biennials and perennials, some of them evergreen. Decorative thistle-like flowers in summer.
Fully to half hardy; **Soil:** Fertile, well-drained; **Position:** Sun
H x S up to 1m x 60cm (3 x 2ft)

Eucalyptus (Gum tree)
Genus of evergreen trees or shrubs. Leaves are round when young, turning oval-oblong when mature. Grown for their bark, flowers and aromatic foliage. Flowers summer to autumn.
Half-hardy; **Soil:** Neutral to acid, moisture-retentive; **Position:** Sun and shelter
H x S up to 30 x 20m (95 x 70ft)

Euonymus fortunei
Prostate to mound-forming evergreen shrub. Leathery leaves. 'Emerald'n'Gold' has vivid yellow margins. 'Emerald Gaiety' has green leaves and white margins.
Fully hardy to frost hardy; **Soil:** Well-drained soil; **Position:** Full sun to light shade. Variegated forms need sun
H x S 5m x indefinite (15ft)

EUPHORBIA
E. characias subsp. **characias**
Evergreen upright shrub. The leaves are strap-shaped and grey-green. Dense spikes of yellowish-green flowers with deep purple centres in spring and early summer.
Frost hardy; **Soil:** Light, well-drained; **Position:** Sun
H 1.2m (4ft)

E. griffithii
Bushy perennial. The leaves are lance-shaped and dark green. Red terminal umbels of flowers in early summer.
Fully hardy; **Soil:** Moist; **Position:** Sun to light shade
H x S 75cm x 1m (30in x 3ft)

E. mellifera (Honey spurge)
Evergreen shrub. Lance-shaped, bright green, veined leaves. Rust-coloured flowers in spring.
Half hardy; **Soil:** Light, well-drained; **Position:** Sun
H x S 1.8 x 2.5m (6 x 8ft)

E. palustris
Bushy perennial. Oblong to lance-shaped, yellowish-green leaves. Clusters of yellow-green flowerheads with cup-shaped bracts appear in spring.
FULLY HARDY; **SOIL:** MOIST BUT WELL-DRAINED; **POSITION:** SUN TO PARTIAL SHADE.
H x S 1m (3ft)

Fatsia japonica
(False castor oil plant)
Evergreen rounded shrub. Large, rounded and deeply lobed leaves. Dense clusters of tiny white flowers in autumn, followed by rounded, black fruits.
FROST HARDY; **SOIL:** FERTILE, MOIST, WELL-DRAINED; **POSITION:** SUN OR SHADE, SHELTERED
H x S 3m (10ft)

Ferula communis
(Giant fennel)
Upright perennial. Finely cut foliage. Large cow parsley-like umbels of yellow flowers borne on tall stems in summer.
FROST HARDY; **SOIL:** FERTILE, WELL-DRAINED; **POSITION:** SUN
H x S 2-3m x 1m (6-10 x 3ft)

Festuca glauca
(Blue fescue grass)
Group of evergreen, tuft-forming, perennial grasses. Narrow leaves in various shades of blue-green to silvery white.
FULLY HARDY; **SOIL:** FERTILE, WELL-DRAINED; **POSITION:** SUN
H x S 30-90 x 10cm (12-30 x 4in)

Fouquiera splendens
(Ocotillo)
Evergreen shrub. Erect canes and insignificant leaves. Spikes of red flowers on leafless stems in summer.
FROST TENDER, MIN. TEMP. 5°C (41°F); **SOIL:** DESERT CONDITIONS; **POSITION:** SUN
H x S 10 x 2m (30 x 6ft)

Griselinia littoralis
(Broadleaf)
Evergreen upright shrub of dense habit. Leathery, rounded apple-green leaves. Tiny inconspicuous yellow flowers in late spring. Wind- and salt-resistant.
FROST HARDY; **SOIL:** LIGHT, WELL-DRAINED; **POSITION:** SUN
H x S 8 x 5m (25 x 15ft)

Gunnera manicata
(Brasilian rhubarb)
Architectural perennial. Rounded, prickly-edged leaves up to 1.5m (5ft) across. Light green flower spikes in early summer, followed by orange-brown seed pods.
HALF-HARDY TO FROST TENDER; **SOIL:** DEEP, MOIST; **POSITION:** SUN TO PARTIAL SHADE. SHELTER FROM WINDS AND PROTECT CROWNS IN WINTER.
H x S 2.5 x 3-4m (8 x 10-13ft)

Hacquetia epipactis
Clump-forming perennial. In late and early spring bears yellow or yellow-green flowerheads, encircled by apple-green bracts, before rounded, 3-parted leaves appear.
FULLY HARDY; **SOIL:** MOIST; **POSITION:** SHADE.
H x S 10 x 15-20cm (4 x 6-8in)

Hakonechloa macra 'Alboaurea'
(Golden Hakone grass)
Slow-growing, herbaceous, perennial grass, with purple stems and green-striped leaves that age to reddish-brown. Open panicles of reddish-brown flower spikes in early autumn may last into the winter.
FULLY HARDY; **SOIL:** RICH, MOIST, WELL-DRAINED; **POSITION:** SUN
H x S 35 x 40cm (14 x 16in)

Helianthus salicifolius
(Willow-leaved sunflower)
Upright perennial. Narrow, willow-like, drooping deep green leaves. Small, daisy-like yellow flowerheads in late summer to early autumn.
FULLY HARDY; **SOIL:** FERTILE, MOIST, WELL-DRAINED; **POSITION:** SUN
H x S 2.5 x 1m (8 x 3ft)

Helleborus argutifolius
(Corsican hellebore)
Evergreen perennial. Tough, well-shaped, dark-green leaves. Cup-shaped flowers in spring. Excellent in woodlands.
FROST HARDY; **SOIL:** MOIST, WELL-DRAINED, NEUTRAL TO ALKALINE; **POSITION:** PARTIAL SHADE
H x S 1.2m x 90cm (4ft x 36in)

Hippophae rhamnoides
(Sea buckthorn)
Deciduous, bushy, arching shrub. Narrow, silvery leaves.

Above: *Helleborus argutifolius*

Tiny yellow flowers in mid-spring, followed by bright orange berries in autumn.
FULLY HARDY; **SOIL:** MOIST, WELL-DRAINED, NEUTRAL TO ALKALINE; **POSITION:** SUN
H x S 6m (18ft)

Hordeum jubatum
(Foxtail barley, Squirreltail grass)
Tufted, short-lived perennial or annual grass. In summer to early autumn has flat, arching, feathery, plume-like flower spikes with silky awns.
FULLY HARDY; **SOIL:** WELL-DRAINED; **POSITION:** FULL SUN
H x S 30-60 x 30cm (1-2 x 1ft)

Hosta
(Plantain lily)
Genus of clump-forming perennials. Grown mainly for their decorative foliage. Flowers in summer.
FULLY HARDY; **SOIL:** FERTILE, MOIST, WELL-DRAINED, NEUTRAL; **POSITION:** FULL TO PARTIAL SHADE
H x S up to 60cm x 1m (2 x 3ft)

Humulus lupulus 'Aureus'
(Golden hop)
Herbaceous, perennial twining climber. Tough, hairy stems and toothed, yellowish vine-shaped leaves.
FULLY HARDY; **SOIL:** MOIST, WELL-DRAINED; **POSITION:** SUN
H 6m (18ft)

HYDRANGEA
H. petiolaris
(Climbing hydrangea)
Deciduous woody climber. Rounded, toothed mid-green leaves. Lacy heads of small, white flowers in summer.
FROST HARDY; **SOIL:** FERTILE, WELL-DRAINED; **POSITION:** SUN TO PARTIAL SHADE
H 15m (50ft)

H. quercifolia
(Oak-leaved hydrangea)
Deciduous, bushy, mound-forming shrub with deeply-lobed, dark green leaves that turn red and purple in autumn. White flower heads are borne from mid-summer to mid-autumn.

FROST HARDY; **SOIL:** MOIST. **POSITION:** PARTIAL SHADE

H x S 1.5 x 2m (5 x 6ft)

Ilex (Holly)

Genus of evergreen trees and shrubs. Grown for their foilage and berries, red to yellow, produced in the autumn.

FULLY TO HALF HARDY; **SOIL:** MOIST, WELL-DRAINED; **POSITION:** SUN OR SEMI-SHADE

H x S Varies according to species.

Inula helenium

(Elecampane)

Clump-forming perennial. Large oval leaves, green on top and silver underneath. Daisy-like yellow flowers on tall stems burst through in summer.

FULLY HARDY; **SOIL:** MOIST, WELL-DRAINED; **POSITION:** SUN TO PARTIAL SHADE

H x S 1-1.8 x 1m (3-6 x 3ft)

IRIS

I. germanica (Bearded iris)

Evergreen, perennial rhizomatous. Leaves are erect and sword-like. Up to 6 yellow, blue-purple or blue-violet bearded flowers on a single stem in late spring to early summer.

FULLY HARDY; **SOIL:** WET OR MOIST SOIL, FREE-DRAINING; **POSITION:** SUN OR SHADE

H 30cm-1m (1-3ft)

I. xiphium (Spanish iris)

Bulbous iris with 1 or 2 blue or violet, occasionally yellow or white flowers, 6-8cm (2.5-3in) across with central, orange or yellow marks on the falls, in spring and early summer. Narrowly lance-shaped, channelled, mid-green leaves.

FULLY HARDY; **SOIL:** WELL-DRAINED; **POSITION:** SUN

H x S 40-60 x 15cm (16-24 x 6in)

Juniperus communis

(Common juniper)

Conifer tree or shrub. Has needle-like, aromatic, glossy leaves and fleshy berries.

FULLY HARDY; **SOIL:** WELL-DRAINED, ALKALINE OR SANDY; **POSITION:** SUN TO PARTIAL SHADE

H x S Varies according to variety.

Right: *Lysichiton americanus*

Kniphofia

(Red-hot poker; Torch lily)

Genus of upright perennials, some evergreen. Flowers borne above grass-like leaves, in summer.

FULLY HARDY; **SOIL:** DEEP, RICH, MOIST, WELL-DRAINED; **POSITION:** FULL SUN

H x S 60cm-1m x 45cm (2-4ft x 18in)

Lavandula (Lavender)

Genus of evergreen shrubs with grey-green, narrow, oblong aromatic leaves. Purple flowers borne on bracts in mid- to late-summer.

FULLY TO HALF HARDY; **SOIL:** WELL-DRAINED; **POSITION:** FULL SUN

H and S 1-1.5m (3-5ft)

LIGULARIA

L. 'Gregynog Gold'

Clump-forming perennial. Leaves are large, heart-shaped and deep green to maroon. Conical panicles of daisy-like, orange-yellow flowers in mid-summer.

FULLY HARDY; **SOIL:** DEEP, MOIST;

POSITION: SUN TO PARTIAL SHADE

H x S 1.8 x 1m (6 x 3ft)

L. stenocephala

Loosely clump-forming perennial with jagged-edged, round, mid-green leaves. Large heads of daisy-like, yellow-orange flowers open on purplish stems from mid- to late summer.

FULLY HARDY; **SOIL:** DEEP, MOIST; **POSITION:** SUN TO PARTIAL SHADE

H x S 1.5-1.8 x 1m (5-6 x 3ft)

Lonicera henryii

Evergreen, woody-stemmed, twining climber. Oblong leaves and fragrant clusters of pink flowers in early summer, followed by black fruit.

FROST HARDY; **SOIL:** WELL-DRAINED; **POSITION:** SUN TO PARTIAL SHADE

H 10m (32ft)

Lyonothamnus floribundus

subsp. **asplenifolius**

(Santa Cruz ironwood)

Slender evergreen tree. Stringy,

reddish-brown bark and fern-like dark green leaves. Large flattened heads of white flowers from spring to summer.

FROST HARDY; **SOIL:** MOIST, WELL-DRAINED; **POSITION:** SUN TO PARTIAL SHADE

H x S 12 x 6m (40 x 18ft)

LYSICHITON

L. americanus

(Yellow skunk cabbage)

Vigorous deciduous, perennial marginal water or bog plant. Produces bright yellow spathes in spring before large green leaves appear.

HALF HARDY; **SOIL:** RICH, AT WATER'S EDGE; **POSITION:** SUN TO PARTIAL SHADE

H x S 1 x 1.2m (3 x 4ft)

L. camtschatcensis

Vigorous, deciduous perennial marginal water or bog plant. Pure white spathes, surrounding spikes of small, insignificant flowers, are borne in spring, before oblong, bright green leaves emerge.

FULLY HARDY; **SOIL:** WET; **POSITION:** FULL SUN.

H x S 75 x 75cm (30 x 30in)

Macleaya microcarpa

(Plume poppy)

Clump-forming perennial. Large, deeply-cut leaves that are deep purple when young, fading to silver-green. Bears large, fluffy panicles of crimson flowers in early summer.

FULLY HARDY; **SOIL:** MOIST, WELL-DRAINED; **POSITION:** SUN

H x S 2.2 x 1m (7 x 3ft)

Magnolia grandiflora

(Bullbay)

Evergreen tree. Large and very fragrant flowers from summer to autumn.

FROST HARDY; **SOIL:** MOIST, WELL-DRAINED, ACID TO NEUTRAL; **POSITION:** SUN TO PARTIAL SHADE

H x S 6-18 x 15m (20-60 x 50ft)

Mahonia

Evergreen shrub. Tough, spiny margined leaves with short racemes of often fragrant, bell-shaped yellow flowers in spring.

FULLY TO HALF HARDY; **SOIL:** MOIST, WELL-DRAINED; **POSITION:** FULL TO PARTIAL SHADE

H x S 1-2.5 x 1.5-4m (3-8 x 5-13ft)

Matteuccia struthiopteris
(Ostrich fern)
Rhizomatous fern with broad
lance-shaped fronds.
HALF HARDY; SOIL: RICH, MOIST, WELL-
DRAINED, NEUTRAL TO ACID; POSITION:
PARTIAL SHADE
H x S 1.5 x 1m (5 x 3ft)

Melianthus major
(Honey flower)
Evergreen, sprawling shrub.
Large, decorative alternate,
pinnate leaves. Brownish-red
flowers in terminal spikes appear
from spring to summer.
FROST TENDER, MIN. TEMP. 5ºC
(41ºF); SOIL: FERTILE, WELL-DRAINED;
POSITION: SUN AND SHELTER
H x S 2 x 3m (6 x 10ft)

Meryta sinclairii
(New Zealand puka)
Evergreen tree. Large, glossy
deep-green veined leaves.
Greenish flowers appear from
spring to autumn, followed by
berry-like black fruits.
FROST TENDER, MIN. TEMP. 5ºC
(41ºF); SOIL: MOIST, RICH; POSITION:
LIGHT SHADE
H x S 8 x 2.5m (25 x 8ft)

**Miscanthus sinensis
'Flamingo'**
(Chinese silver grass)
Perennial grass. Flowers in
autumn.
HALF-HARDY; SOIL: MOIST, WELL-
DRAINED; POSITION: SUN
H x S 1.5 x 1.2m (5 x 4ft)

Molinia caerulea ssp.
arundinacea 'Transparent'
(Purple moor-grass)
Perennial grass. Flowers in
autumn.
FULLY HARDY; SOIL: MOIST, WELL-
DRAINED; POSITION: SUN
H x S 1.8 x 1m (6 x 3ft)

Musa basjoo
(Japanese banana)
Evergreen, palm-like, suckering
perennial with arching leaves up
to 1m (3ft) long. Has drooping,
pale yellow flowers with
brownish bracts in summer,
followed by green fruits.
HALF HARDY; SOIL: WELL-DRAINED.
POSITION: FULL SUN
H x S 3-5 x 2-2.5m
(10-15 x 6-8ft)

Right: *Melianthus major*

Nandina domestica
(Heavenly bamboo)
Semi-evergreen shrub. Lance-
shaped delicate leaves, coloured
reddish when new. Large
panicles of small, white flowers
in summer, followed by berries.
FULLY HARDY; SOIL: MOIST, WELL-
DRAINED; POSITION: SUN AND SHELTER
H x S 45cm-1.5m x 60cm-1.2m
(18in-5ft x 2-4ft)

Nymphaea (Water lily)
Genus of acquatic perennials.
Smooth rounded leaves. Flowers
in summer. N. 'Candida' is a
white variety for water 15-25cm
(6-12in) deep; N. 'Caroliniana
Nivea', with double, scented
white flowers, for water
25-75cm (12-30in) deep;
N. 'Gladstoneana', with large
white fragrant flowers, for water
30cm-1m (1-3ft) deep.
FULLY HARDY TO FROST TENDER;
SOIL: UNDISTURBED WATER, LOAMY;
POSITION: SUN
H x S varies according to variety.

Olea europea var. **europea**
(Edible olive)
Evergreen tree. Leathery, oblong
leaves are grey-green above,
silvery beneath. Tiny, fragrant
white flowers in summer are
followed by edible green and
later purple fruits in autumn.
HALF-HARDY TO TENDER; SOIL: DEEP,
WELL-DRAINED; POSITION: SUN
H 10m (32ft)

**ONOPORDUM
O. acanthium**
(Scotch thistle)
Slow-growing, erect biennial.
Leaves are silvery-grey, large
and sharply defined. Stems bear
purple-pink flowerheads in
summer.
FULLY HARDY; SOIL: FERTILE, WELL-
DRAINED, ALKALINE TO NEUTRAL;
POSITION: SUN
H x S 2.5 x 1m (8 x 3ft)

O. nervosum
Biennial, similar to above.
FULLY HARDY; SOIL: FERTILE, WELL-

DRAINED, ALKALINE TO NEUTRAL;
POSITION: SUN
H x S 2.5 x 1m (8 x 3ft)

Ophiopogon
(Snake's beard)
Genus of evergreen perennials.
Strap-like leaves. Racemes of
flowers in summer.
FULLY TO HALF HARDY; SOIL: MOIST,
WELL-DRAINED, SLIGHTLY ACID;
POSITION: SUN TO PARTIAL SHADE
H x S 15-60 x 30cm (6-24 x 12in)

Osmunda regalis
(Royal Fern)
Deciduous fern with bright green
fronds. Rust-brown flower spikes
at ends of taller fronds in
summer.
FULLY HARDY; SOIL: WET, ACID;
POSITION: SUN TO PARTIAL SHADE
H x S 2 x 1m (6 x 3ft)

Panicum virgatum
(Switch grass)
Perennial grass. Flowers in
autumn.
FULLY HARDY; SOIL: WELL-DRAINED;
POSITION: SUN
H x S 1.2m x 60cm (4 x 2ft)

Paulownia
Genus of deciduous trees. Large
ovate green to yellow-green
leaves. Lilac flowers in late
spring.
FULLY HARDY; SOIL: FERTILE, WELL-
DRAINED; POSITION: SUN
H x S 12 x 10m (40 x 32ft)

Phillyrea latifolia
(Jasmine box)
Evergreen rounded shrub or
tree. Leaves are oval, glossy,
dark green. Tiny, fragrant, white
flowers in late spring to summer.
HALF HARDY; SOIL: FERTILE, WELL-
DRAINED; POSITION: SUN
H 8m (25ft)

Phormium tenax
Evergreen upright perennial.
Tufts of sword-shaped, stiff dark
green leaves. Panicles of tubular,
dull-red flowers are produced on
short, slightly glaucous stems in
summer. Thrives by the sea.
FROST TENDER, MIN. TEMP. 10-15ºC
(50-59ºF); SOIL: FERTILE, WELL-
DRAINED; POSITION: SUN TO PARTIAL
SHADE
H x S 3 x 1-1.8m (10 x 3-6ft)

PHYLLOSTACHYS
P. nigra
(Black bamboo)
Evergreen bamboo. Stems turn
black in the second or third year
with lance-shaped green leaves.
FROST HARDY; **SOIL:** MOIST, RICH,
WELL-DRAINED; **POSITION:** SUN TO
SHADE
H x S 6-8 x 2-3m (18-25 x 6-10ft)

P. vivax 'Aureocaulis'
Evergreen bamboo. Thick canes
with rich, yellow random stripes.
FULLY HARDY; **SOIL:** MOIST, RICH, WELL-
DRAINED; **POSITION:** SUN TO SHADE
H x S 8 x 1.8-3m (24 x 6-10ft)

Pleioblastus auricomus
Evergreen, slow-spreading
bamboo with wonderful yellow
leaves with green stripes and
purple-green slender culms.
FULLY HARDY; **SOIL:** WELL-DRAINED;
POSITION: FULL LIGHT
H up to 1.5m (5ft)

PINUS
P. mugo (Dwarf mountain pine)
Evergreen spreading conifer.
Needle-like dark green leaves.
HARDY TO HALF HARDY; **SOIL:** WELL-
DRAINED; **POSITION:** SUN
H x S 3.5 x 5m (11 x 15ft)

P. nigra (Austrian pine)
Evergreen conifer. Dense head of
branches with dark green,
needle-like leaves. Good in
maritime situations, a sturdy
wind-break.
HARDY TO HALF HARDY; **SOIL:** WELL-
DRAINED, CHALK TOLERANT; **POSITION:**
SUN
H x S 30 x 6-8m (100ft x 20-25ft)

P. taeda (Loblolly pine)
Evergreen conifer. Glaucous
young shoots and slender,
needle-like leaves.
HALF HARDY; **SOIL:** WELL-DRAINED;
POSITION: SUN TO PARTIAL SHADE
H x S 10m (32ft)

PITTOSPORUM
P. 'Garnettii'
Evergreen shrub. Silver-green,
margined cream leaves with
brown, insignificant flowers in
spring.
HALF HARDY; **SOIL:** MOIST, WELL-
DRAINED; **POSITION:** SUN TO PARTIAL
SHADE
H x S 3-5 x 2-4m (10-15 x 6-12ft)

Above: *Rodgersia podophylla* and *Iris pseudacorus* 'Variegata'

P. tobira
(Japanese mock orange)
Evergreen rounded shrub. Leaves
are deep green, with a lighter
underside. Scented umbels of
cream flowers in summer.
HALF HARDY; **SOIL:** WELL-DRAINED;
POSITION: SUN
H x S 6 x 1.5-3m (18 x 5-10ft)

Plantago major var.
atropurpurea
(Great purple plantain)
Evergreen perennial. Club-
shaped maroon leaves with
insignificant flowers.
HARDY; **SOIL:** WELL-DRAINED; **POSITION:**
SUN TO PARTIAL SHADE
H x S 20 x 20cm (8 x 8in)

Pontederia cordata
(Pickerel weed)
Marginal aquatic perennial.
Large spear-shaped glossy leaves
and blue flowers in summer.
FULLY HARDY; **SOIL:** WET, LOAMY;
POSITION: FULL SUN
H x S 1.3m x 75cm (52 x 30in)

PRUNUS
P. 'Spire'
Vase-shaped tree. Dark green
leaves turning to orange-red in
autumn. Pink flowers in spring.
HARDY; **SOIL:** MOIST, WELL-DRAINED;
POSITION: SUN
H x S 10 x 6m (32 x 20ft)

P. laurocerasus (Cherry laurel)
Evergreen shrub. Glossy, oblong
leaves. Fragrant flowers in late
spring, followed by cherry-like
fruit.
HARDY; **SOIL:** MOIST, WELL-DRAINED;
POSITION: SUN
H x S 8 x 10m (25 x 32ft)

P. lusitanica (Portugal laurel)
Evergreen shrub. Dark green,
ovate leaves, with scented
flowers in spring.
HALF HARDY; **SOIL:** MOIST, WELL-

DRAINED; **POSITION:** SUN
H 20m (70ft)

P. shirotae 'Mount Fuji'
Deciduous tree. Pale green
leaves turning to orange in
autumn. Double, scented flowers
in spring.
HARDY; **SOIL:** MOIST, WELL-DRAINED;
POSITION: SUN
H x S 6 x 8m (18 x 25ft)

P. x yedoensis 'Ivensii'
(Yoshino cherry)
Deciduous tree. Dark green
leaves and pale pink flowers in
spring.
HARDY; **SOIL:** MOIST, WELL-DRAINED;
POSITION: SUN
H x S 15 x 10m (50 x 30ft)

Pseudosasa japonica
Upright culms. Leaves medium to
large.
HARDY; **SOIL:** MOIST, WELL-DRAINED;
POSITION: SUN TO PARTIAL SHADE
H 6m (20ft)

Pulmonaria (Lungwort)
Genus of mainly spring-flowering
perennials, some semi-evergreen.
Blue-green leaves with silver
marking and pink or blue flowers.
FULLY HARDY; **SOIL:** FERTILE, WELL-
DRAINED; **POSITION:** SHADE
H x S 30 x 45cm (12 x 18in)

Rhamnus alaternus
'Argenteovariegata'
(Buckthorn)
Evergreen shrub. Leaves are
grey-green with a cream margin.
Insignificant flowers in spring.
FROST HARDY; **SOIL:** FERTILE; **POSITION:**
SUN TO PARTIAL SHADE
H x S 5 x 4m (15 x 13ft)

Rhapis (Lady palm)
Genus of evergreen palms.
Leaves are light to mid-green,
arranged in groups on stems.
FROST TENDER, MIN. TEMP. 15°C
(59°F); **SOIL:** MOIST, FERTILE, WELL-
DRAINED; **POSITION:** LIGHT SHADE
H 1.5-5m (5-15ft)

Rodgersia
Genus of clump-forming
perennials. Large, well-shaped
leaves on long stems, turning
bronze in autumn. White-pink
flowers in summer.
HARDY; **SOIL:** MOIST, FERTILE; **POSITION:**
SUN TO PARTIAL SHADE
H x S 60cm x 1.8m (2 x 6ft)

Rubus phoenicolasius
(Japanese wineberry)
Woody climber. Trifoliate mid-green leaves turning yellow in autumn. Blackberry-like flowers in summer followed by blackberry-like fruits in autumn.
HALF HARDY; **SOIL:** WELL-DRAINED; **POSITION:** LIGHT SHADE
H 3m (10ft)

Sansevieria trifasciata 'Laurentii'
(Mother-in-law's tongue)
Evergreen perennial. Rosettes of stiff, stemless, pointed, green and yellow leaves.
FROST TENDER, MIN. TEMP. 15°C (59°F); **SOIL:** POOR, FREELY-DRAINING, NEUTRAL TO ALKALINE; **POSITION:** SUN
H x S 1m x 20cm (3ft x 8in)

Santolina
Genus of evergreen, summer-flowering shrubs, grown for their aromatic foliage and their button-like flowerheads, each on a long stem.
FROST HARDY; **SOIL:** NOT TOO RICH, WELL-DRAINED; **POSITION:** SUN
H x S 75cm x 1m (2.5 x 3ft)

Schefflera actinophylla
(Queensland umbrella tree)
Erect tree with large and divided glossy bright green leaves, borne in rosettes.
FROST TENDER, MIN. TEMP. 16°C (61°F); **SOIL:** MOIST, FERTILE, WELL-DRAINED; **POSITION:** LIGHT SHADE
H x S 12 x 6m (40 x 18ft)

Sedum
Genus of succulent annual, biennual and perennial semi-evergreen or evergreen shrubs.
FULLY HARDY TO FROST TENDER, MIN. TEMP. 5°C (41°F); **SOIL:** ANY, BUT BEST IN FERTILE, WELL-DRAINED SOIL; **POSITION:** SUN
H up to 45cm (18in)

Semiarundinaria fastuosa
(Narihira bamboo)
Evergreen clump-forming bamboo. Mid-green canes, striped purple when young.
HARDY; **SOIL:** MOIST, FERTILE, WELL-DRAINED; **POSITION:** SUN
H x S 7 x 1.8m (21 x 6ft)

Sempervivum (House leek)
Genus of evergreen, clump-forming succulents. Stout, green or red fleshy leaves.

FULLY HARDY; **SOIL:** POOR, WELL DRAINED; **POSITION:** SUN
H x S 8 x 30cm (3 x 12in)

Shibataea lancefolia
(Short bamboo)
Evergreen, clump-forming bamboo. Thin long culms with good medium leaves.
FULLY HARDY; **SOIL:** FERTILE, WELL-DRAINED; **POSITION:** SUN
H up to 1.5m (5ft)

SORBUS
S. aria 'Lutescens'
(Whitebeam)
Deciduous, spreading tree. Young leaves are silvery, maturing to grey-green. Small white clusters of flowers in spring, followed by orange-red berries.
FULLY HARDY; **SOIL:** FERTILE, WELL-DRAINED; **POSITION:** SUN
H x S 15 x 10m (50 x 32ft)

S. aucuparia (Mountain ash)
Deciduous, rounded to conical tree. Leaves are lance-shaped and dark-green, with vibrant autumn colours. White flowers in spring, red fruit in autumn.
FULLY HARDY; **SOIL:** FERTILE, WELL-DRAINED; **POSITION:** SUN
H x S 15 x 7m (50 x 21ft)

Stachys byzantina
(Lamb's ears)
Evergreen, mat-forming perennial excellent for ground cover. Greyish-green, oblong, felted leaves. Insignificant mauve-pink flowers in summer.
FULLY HARDY; **SOIL:** WELL-DRAINED; **POSITION:** SUN
H x S 45 x 60cm (18 x 24in)

Stipa gigantea (Golden oats)
Evergreen, tuft-forming perennial grass with narrow leaves. Open panicles of silvery spikelets with long dangling golden anthers which persist well into winter.
FROST HARDY; **SOIL:** LIGHT, WELL-DRAINED; **POSITION:** SUN
H x S 2.5 x 1.2m (8 x 4ft)

Stratiotes aloides
(Water soldier)
Semi-evergreen aquatic perennial. Toothed, sword-like green leaves borne in rosettes. Cup-shaped white flowers in summer.
FULLY HARDY; **SOIL:** WET; **POSITION:** SUN TO PARTIAL SHADE
S 26cm (10in)

Above: *Stipa gigantea*

Strelitzia nicolai
Evergreen, clump-forming perennial. Stout trunk and 1.5m (5ft) or more long, paddle-shaped leaves. Beak-like white and pale blue flowers in spring.
FROST TENDER, MIN. TEMP. 5-10°C (41-50°F); **SOIL:** WELL-DRAINED, FERTILE; **POSITION:** PARTIAL SHADE
H x S 10 x 5m (32 x 15ft)

Styrax obassia
(Fragrant snowbell)
Columnar tree. Rounded leaves, yellow in autumn. White bell-shaped flowers from early to mid-summer.
FROST HARDY; **SOIL:** MOIST, RICH, NEUTRAL TO ACID; **POSITION:** SUN TO PARTIAL SHADE. SHELTER FROM WINDS
H x S 12 x 7m (40 x 21ft)

Tamarix ramoissima
(Tamarisk)
Deciduous, graceful shrub. Insignificant, tiny, blue-green leaves. Large plumes of small pink flowers in late summer and early autumn.

FULLY HARDY; **SOIL:** WELL-DRAINED, LIGHT, SANDY; **POSITION:** SUN
H 5m (15ft)

Taxus baccata (Yew)
Slow-growing conifer with a broadly conical, later domed crown. Needle-like, flattened leaves are dark green.
FULLY HARDY; **SOIL:** ANY; **POSITION:** SHADE TOLERANT
H x S 12 x 8m (40 x 25ft)

TRACHYCARPUS
T. fortunei
(Chusan palm, Windmill palm)
Evergreen palm. Fan-shaped leaves. Sprays of fragrant, creamy flowers in early summer.
FROST HARDY; **SOIL:** FERTILE, WELL-DRAINED; **POSITION:** SUN TO LIGHT SHADE AND SHELTER
H x S 20 x 2.5m (70 x 8ft)

T. latisectus
(Windermere palm)
Fast-growing, evergreen palm. Large, leathery fan-shaped leaves and bare trunk.

FROST HARDY; SOIL: FERTILE, WELL-
DRAINED; POSITION: SUN AND
SHELTERED FROM WIND
H x S 6 x 3m (20 x 10ft)

Trichocereus
Genus of columnar, perennial
cacti. Mature plants produce
highly scented nocturnal funnel-
shaped flowers that eventually
open flat.
FROST TENDER, MIN. TEMP. 8-10ºC
(46-50º F); SOIL: WELL-DRAINED;
POSITION: SUN
H x S 5 x 1m (15 x 3ft)

TRILLIUM
T. grandiflorum
(American wood lily)
Clump-forming perennial. Club-
shaped dark green leaves. Large
white flowers from spring to
summer.
FULLY HARDY; SOIL: MOIST, WELL-
DRAINED, ACID TO NEUTRAL; POSITION:
SHADE
H x S 40 x 30cm (16 x 12in)

T. sessile (Toadshade)
Clump-forming perennial. Club-
shaped marbled leaves. Red-
brown flowers in spring.
FULLY HARDY; SOIL: MOIST, WELL-
DRAINED, ACID TO NEUTRAL; POSITION:
PARTIAL SHADE
H x S 35 x 40cm (14 x 16in)

Tropaeolum speciosum
(Flame nasturtium)
Herbaceous, twining perennial
climber. Lobed mid-green leaves
and scarlet flowers in summer,
followed by bright blue fruits.
FULLY HARDY; SOIL: MOIST, WELL-
DRAINED, NEUTRAL TO ACID; POSITION:
ROOTS IN SHADE, HEAD IN SUN
H 3m (10ft)

VERBASCUM
V. bombyciferum
Evergreen, erect biennial. Oval
leaves and stems covered with
silver hairs. Has upright racemes
densely set with 5-lobed, yellow
flowers in summer.
FULLY HARDY; SOIL: WELL-DRAINED;
POSITION: SUN TO PARTIAL SHADE
H X S 1.2-1.8m x 60cm (4-6 x 2ft)

V. olympicum
Semi-evergreen, short-lived
perennial, usually grown as a
biennial. Upright stems arising
from felt-like grey foliage at base
of plant. Sprays of 5-lobed

yellow flowers in summer to
autumn.
FULLY HARDY; SOIL: ALKALINE, POOR;
POSITION: SUN
H x S 1.8 x 1m (6 x 3ft)

V. thapsus
(Great mullein)
Upright semi-evergreen biennial.
Leaves in white-grey rosettes.
Yellow flowers in summer.
FULLY HARDY; SOIL: WELL-DRAINED,
ALKALINE, POOR; POSITION: SUN
H x S 1.8 x 1m (6 x 3ft)

Verbena bonariensis
Perennial with basal clump of
dark green, insignificant leaves.
Upright stems carry tufts of purple
flowers in summer and autumn.
FULLY HARDY; SOIL: WELL-DRAINED;
POSITION: SUN
H x S 2m x 45cm (6ft x 18in)

VIBURNUM
V. plicatum 'Rowallane'
Compact shrub. Heart-shaped
green leaves, with vibrant
autumn colour. Flowers in
summer, followed by red fruits in
autumn.

Above: *Yucca gloriosa, verbena* and *melianthus*

FULLY HARDY; SOIL: MOIST, WELL-
DRAINED; POSITION: SUN TO PARTIAL
SHADE
H 2m (6ft)

V. tinus (Laurustinus)
Evergreen dense shrub. Dark
green oval leaves. Flat heads of
small white flowers in late winter
and spring.
FROST HARDY; SOIL: MOIST, WELL-
DRAINED; POSITION: SUN
H x S 3 x 3m (10 x 10ft)

Vitis coignetiae
(Crimson glory vine)
Deciduous, vigorous woody
climber. Large, heart-shaped
leaves with good autumn colour.
Flowers insignificant.
FULLY HARDY; SOIL: WELL-DRAINED,
NEUTRAL TO ALKALINE; POSITION: SUN
TO PARTIAL SHADE
H 6m (18ft)

Wisteria floribunda
(Japanese wisteria)
Deciduous, woody-stemmed,
twining climber. Pinnate, mid-
green leaflets. Scented, drooping
racemes of flowers in early
summer.
FULLY HARDY; SOIL: FERTILE, MOIST,
WELL-DRAINED; POSITION: SUN
H 9m (28ft)

Xanthosoma sagittifolium
(Yautia)
Wide-spreading, tufted
perennial. Broad, spear-shaped
leaves, which may also be
spotted, on long stalks.
FROST TENDER, MIN. TEMP. 15ºC
(59ºF); SOIL: MOIST, RICH; POSITION:
SUN TO PARTIAL SHADE
H x S 1.8m (6ft)

Yucca gloriosa
(Adam's needle)
Evergreen shrub. Tufts of lance-
shaped, deep green leaves, blue-
green when young. Bell-shaped
white flowers from summer to
autumn.
FULLY HARDY; SOIL: WELL-DRAINED;
POSITION: SUN
H x S 2.5 x 1.8m (8 x 6ft)

Zea 'Hungarian red'
Annual corn. Lance-shaped
green leaves. Reddish flowers in
loose panicles in autumn.
HALF HARDY; SOIL: WARM, WELL-
DRAINED; POSITION: SUN AND SHELTER
H 1.2m (4ft)

RESOURCES

USEFUL ADDRESSES

UK

Apple Court
Hordle Lane,
Hordle, Lymington,
Hampshire SO41 0HU
Tel: (01590) 642 130
*National Reference Collection of
Small-leafed Hosta.
Specializes in Hostas and
Grasses*

Architectural Plants
Cook's Farm, Nuthurst, Horsham,
West Sussex
Tel: (01403) 891 772
*Specialize in exotics and
architectural natives*

Cotswold Garden Flowers
Sands Lane, Badsey, Evesham,
Worcestershire
Tel: (01386) 422 829
*Specializes in unusual plants
Mail Order service*

Drysdale Garden Exotics
Bowerwood Road,
Fordingbridge, Hampshire
SP6 1BN
Tel: (01425) 653 010
*National Reference Collection of
Bamboos - specialist nursery*

European Boxwood & Topiary
Society
The Dower House, Crimp Hill
Old Windsor, Berkshire
SL14 2HL
Tel: (01753) 854 982

The Hardy Plant Society
Administrator: Mrs. Pam Adams
Little Orchard, Great Comberton,
Pershore, Worcestershire
WR10 3DP

The Palm Centre
Ham Nursery, Ham Street, Ham,
Richmond, Surrey TW10 7HA
Tel: (020) 8255 6191

Royal Horticultural Society
PO Box 313, Vincent Square,
London SW1P 2PE
Tel: (020) 7834 4333

Spinners Nursery
School Lane Boldre, Lymington,
Hampshire SO41 5QE
Tel: (01590) 673 347
*Trillium, Ferns, Rodgersia and
unusual woodland plants*

www.e-garden.co.uk
*For buying online and gardening
advice*

USA

Cactus & Succulent Society
of America
PO Box 2615, Pahrump,
NV 89041-2615
Tel: (001) 702 751 1351

Japanese Garden Society
of Oregon
PO Box 3847, Portland,
Oregon 97208

SOUTH AFRICA

Keith Kirsten's Bedfordview
Nursery
92 Concorde Road East,
Bedfordview 2007
Tel: (011) 455 4000
Fax: (011) 455 6361

Lifestyle Family Garden Centre
Corner of DF Malan and
Ysterhout Avenue, PO Box 2568,
Northcliff 2115
Tel: (011) 792 5616
Fax: (011) 792 5626

Dunrobin Garden Pavillion
Old Main Road, Botha's Hill
Tel: (031) 777 1855
Fax: (031) 777 1893

Botanical Society of South Africa
Kirstenbosch, Cape Town 7735
Tel: (021) 797 2090

The Garden Centre
Kirstenbosch Botanical Gardens,
PO Box 195, Newlands 7725
Tel: (021) 762 1621
Fax: (021) 762 0923

Grey Heron Nurseries
Langeberg Road, Langeberg
Ridge, Durbanville
Tel: (021) 988 7670 or
(021) 988 9124
Fax: (021) 988 7670

Sheilam Cactus Nursery
PO Box 157, Robertson 6705
Tel: (023) 626 4133
Fax: (023) 626 4133

AUSTRALIA

*For advice on unusual plants and
information about nurseries
contact the following
organisations:*

Nursery Industry of Australia Ltd
16-18 Cambridge, Epping
NSW 2121
Tel: (02) 9876 5200
Fax: (02) 9876 6360

Nursery Industry Association
of NSW
PO Box 13, Rouse Hill,
New South Wales 2155
Tel: (02) 9679 1472

Nursery Industry Association of
Northern Territory Inc.
PO Box 40, Humpty Doo,
Northern Territory 0893
Tel: (08) 8988 1351

Nursery Industry Association
of Victoria
PO Box 431, Caulfield East,
Victoria 3145
Tel: (03) 9576 0599

Nursery Industry Association
of Tasmania
PO Box 17, Launceston,
Tasmania 7250
Tel: (03) 6398 2474

Nursery Industry Association of
Western Australia
Fraser Avenue, Kings Park,
Western Australia 6005
Tel: (08) 9485 1144

Queensland Nursery Industry
Association
PO Box 345, Salisbury,
Queensland 4107
Tel: (07) 3277 7900

Nursery and Landscape Industry
of South Australia
136 Greenhill Road, Unley,
South Australia 5061
Tel: (08) 8300 0172

NEW ZEALAND

Palmers Garden Centres
Head Office:
182 Wairau Road,
Glenfield, Auckland
Tel: (09) 443 9910
(Branches nationwide)

Kings Plant Barn
(Auckland only)
Takapuna, tel: (09) 443 2221
Remuera, tel: (09) 524 9400
St Lukes, tel: (09) 846 2141
Howick, tel: (09) 273 8527

FRANCE

Societé Nationale d'Horticulture
de France
84 rue de Grenelle, Paris
F-75007
Tel: (0033) 1 44 39 78 78

BIBLIOGRAPHY

Anderson, M. *The Ultimate Book of Cacti & Succulents*, Lorenz Books, 1998

Australian Gardening Encyclopaedia, Random House, 1998

Brookes, J. *John Brookes' Garden Design Book*, Dorling Kindersley, 1991

Brown, J. *Lanning Roper and His Gardens*, Weidenfeld & Nicolson, 1987

Brown, J. *The Art and Architecture of English Gardens*, Weidenfeld & Nicolson, 1989

Chatterton, J. *Grasses*, Lorenz Books, 1998

Chatto, B. *The Green Tapestry*, Collins, 1989

Clarke, E. *Leaf, Bark & Berry*, David & Charles, 1999

Davies, B. *The Gardener's Essential Plant Guide*, Laurel Glen Publishing, 1997

Dickey, P. *Breaking Ground*, Artisan, 1997

Fearnley-Whittingstall, J. *Ivies*, Chatto & Windus, 1992

Gilemeister, H. *Meddisterranean Gardening*, Editorial Moll, 1998

Grenfell, D. *The Plant Finder's Guide to Growing Hostas*, David & Charles, 1996

Grounds, R. *The Plant Finder's Guide to Ornamental Grasses*, David & Charles/ Timber Press, 1998

Harte, S. *Zen Gardening*, Pavilion/Stewart Tabori & Chang, 1999

Hendy, J. *Quick & Easy Topiary and Green Sculpture*, Little Brown & Company, 1998

Hillier Gardener's Guide to Trees & Shrubs, The, David & Charles, 1995

Hobhouse, P. *Penelope Hobhouse on Gardening*, Frances Lincoln, 1994

King, M. & Oudolf, P. *Gardening with Grasses*, Frances Lincoln, 1998

Masson, G. *Italian Gardens*, Thames & Hudson, 1961

Page, R. *The Education of a Gardener*, Harvill, 1994

Perry, F. A. *Collins Guide to Waterlilies and other Aquatic Plants*, Collins, 1988

Power, N. G. *The Gardens of California*, Thames and Hudson, 1995

Putnam, G. P. *The Art of Zen Gardens*, Tarcher/Putnam Books, 1983

R.H.S. A - Z Encyclopaedia of Garden Plants, The, Dorling Kindersley, 1996

R.H.S. Plant Finder, The, Dorling Kindersley, published annually

Rice, G. & Strangman, E. *The Gardener's Guide to Growing Hellebores*, David & Charles, 1993

Seike, K. & Kudo, M. *A Japanese Touch for your Garden*, Kodansha International, 1992

Strong, R. *The Small Garden Designers Handbook*, Conran Octopus, 1987

Taylor, G. & Cooper, G. *Gardens of Obsession*, Weidenfeld & Nicolson, 1999

Taylor, G. & Cooper, G. *Paradise Transformed*, The Monacelli Press, 1996

Thomas, G. S. *Ornamental Shrubs, Climbers & Bamboos*, John Murray, 1992

Thomas, G. S. *Perennial Garden Plants*, Dent, 1993

Truelove, J. G. *The New American Garden*, Whitney Library of Design, 1998

Valery, M. *Gardens of France*, Taschen, 1997

Walker, J. *The Subtropical Garden*, Godwit Press Ltd, 1992

INDEX

ACKNOWLEDGMENTS

I would like to thank Yvonne McFarlane of New Holland Publishers for asking me to write this book, a subject that is close to my heart, and Pat White who negotiated on my behalf. Thanks also to Rosemary Wilkinson for guiding me through the initial stages and to Christine Rista, my chief editor, who has always been a delight to work with. Roger Hammond has designed a book that is a visual pleasure, so thank you to him. I am also grateful to all those gardeners and nurserymen who, throughout the years, have generously shared their knowledge with me.

PHOTOGRAPHIC CREDITS

1 GPL/Ron Sutherland; 2 GPL/JS Sira; 4-5 Sunniva Harte; 6 (top left) Jonathan Buckley; 6 (centre) Andrew Lawson; 6 (bottom right) Andrew Lawson; 6-7 (top) Jerry Harpur/La Casella, Alpes-Martimes; 7 (top right) Sunniva Harte; 8 Jerry Harpur, des: Mary Effran, Santa Monica, Ca; 9 John Glover; 10-11 Jerry Harpur/La Casella, Alpes-Martimes; 12 (top) Jerry Harpur/Clos du Peyronnet, Menton; 12 (centre) John Glover; 12-13 Clive Nichols, des: Claus Scheinert; 14 GPL/Ron Sutherland; 14-15 GPL/Steven Wooster; 16-17 John Glover; 17 Andrew Lawson; 18-19 Clive Nichols, des: Anne Waring; 20-21 Jerry Harpur/Villa Cetinale, Italy; 22-23 GPL/Brigitte Thomas; 23 John Glover; 24 John Glover; 25 Sunniva Harte; 26-27 Jonathan Buckley; 27 Sunniva Harte; 29 Jonathan Buckley; 30-31 Jerry Harpur/La Casella, Alpes-Martimes; 31 (top right) GPL/Ron Sutherland; 31 (centre right) Jerry Harpur/La Casella, Alpes-Martimes; 32 Jerry Harpur/Mr & Mrs Lemer, Palm Springs, Ca; 32-33 Clive Nichols/Huntington Botanical Gardens, USA; 33 Clive Nichols/Huntington Botanical Gardens, USA; 34 Jerry Harpur, des: Mado Wijaya, Singapore; 35 Sunniva Harte; 36 Jerry Harpur, des:

Terry Welch, Seattle, Wa; 38 Jerry Harpur/Mrs Pomeroy, Ca; 39 Sunniva Harte; 40 Jerry Harpur/Titoki Point, Taihape, NZ; 41 Andrew Lawson; 42-43 GPL/JS Sira; 44-45 Clive Nichols, des: Denmans/John Brookes; 46 Jonathan Buckley; 47 Clive Nichols, des: Beth Chatto Garden, Essex; 48 GPL/Brigitte Thomas; 49 GPL/Lamontagne; 50-51 Jerry Harpur/La Casella, Alpes-Martimes; 53 John Glover; 54-55 Jerry Harpur/La Casella, Alpes-Martimes; 56-57 Jerry Harpur, des: Wolfgang Oehme and Jim Van Sweden; 58 Clive Nichols/Huntington Botanical Gardens, USA; 58-59 Jerry Harpur/La Casella, Alpes-Martimes; 59 Jerry Harpur/Royal Botanic Garden, Singapore; 60-61 Clive Nichols/The Old Vicarage, Norfolk; 61 (top) Jonathan Buckley; 61 (centre) Clive Nichols/Villandry, France; 62 Andrew Lawson; 62-63 Jonathan Buckley; 64 GPL/Ron Sutherland; 65 Sunniva Harte; 66 Sunniva Harte; 67 Sunniva Harte; 68-69 GPL/JS Sira; 70-71 GPL/Ron Sutherland; 73 GPL/Steven Wooster; 74-75 Sunniva Harte; 76 GPL/Eric Crichton; 76-77 Sunniva Harte; 78 John Glover; 79 (top left) Andrew Lawson/Waddeson Manor, Bucks; 79 (centre right)

GPL/Howard Rice; 80-81 GPL/Marijke Heuff; 82 Andrew Lawson; 83 Andrew Lawson; 84 Jonathan Buckley; 84-85 John Glover; 86-87 John Glover; 87 Clive Nichols, des: Dennis Fairweather; 88-89 Andrew Lawson/Sticky Wicket, Dorset; 89 Sunniva Harte; 90 Jonathan Buckley; 90-91 Jonathan Buckley; 92-93 Andrew Lawson; 94-95 GPL/Brigitte Thomas; 96-97 GPL/Brigitte Thomas; 97 Clive Nichols, des: Henk Gerritsen; 98-99 Jonathan Buckley; 100 Jerry Harpur/La Casella, Alpes-Martimes; 101 GPL/John Glover; 102 Sunniva Harte; 102-103 Jerry Harpur/Les Quatres Vents, La Malbaie, Quebec; 103 (top right) Clive Nichols, des: Claus Scheinert; 103 (centre) Jerry Harpur/Clos du Peyronnet, Menton; 104 Andrew Lawson; 104-105 GPL/Ron Sutherland; 106-107 Andrew Lawson/Bourton House, Gloucestershire; 108 Jerry Harpur/The Japanese Garden, Portland, Or; 109 (left) Jerry Harpur, des: Mrs Pomeroy, Ca; 109 (right) Sunniva Harte; 110 Sunniva Harte; 111 Andrew Lawson; 112 Andrew Lawson/Rofford Manor, Oxford; 113 GPL/Brigitte Thomas; 114 Sunniva Harte; 115 Clive Nichols; 116-117 GPL/John Glover; 117

Jerry Harpur; 118-119 Clive Nichols, des: David Hicks; 120 Andrew Lawson, des: Mirabel Osler; 120-121 GPL/John Glover; 122-123 GPL/Steven Wooster; 123 Clive Nichols; 124 John Glover; 125 Andrew Lawson/Stone Lane Gardens, Chagford, Devon; 126 GPL/Howard Rice; 127 GPL/Neil Holmes; 128-129 Jonathan Buckley; 130 Clive Nichols/Strybing Arboretum, Ca; 131 Jerry Harpur/La Casella, Alpes-Martimes; 132 Sunniva Harte; 133 Sunniva Harte; 134 GPL/Brian Carter; 135 GPL/Sunniva Harte; 136 Sunniva Harte; 137 Sunniva Harte; 138 GPL/Brian Carter; 139 Sunniva Harte

Front Cover: John Glover/Wisley, Surrey. Back Cover: Jerry Harpur, des: Mary Effran, GPL/JS Sira. Front Flap: Jerry Harpur/La Casella, Alpes-Maritimes. Back Flap: Robert Jacob. Spine Detail: Clive Nichols, des: Denmans/John Brookes.